W9-BGH-655

MODE IN JAVANESE MUSIC

MODE IN JAVANESE MUSIC

by

Susan Pratt Walton

Ohio University Center for International Studies
Monographs in International Studies

Southeast Asia Series Number 79
Athens, Ohio 1987

Illustrations taken from
Traditional Music in Modern Java
by Judith Becker (Honolulu: The University Press of Hawaii, 1980).
Used by Permission.

Library of Congress Cataloging-in-Publication Data

Walton, Susan Pratt.
    Mode in Javanese music.

    (Monographs in international studies. Southeast
Asia series; no. 79)
    Bibliography: p.
    1. Music—Indonesia—Java—History and criticism.
2. Musical intervals and scales. 3. Gamelan. I. Title.
II. Series.
ML345.I5W3   1987   781'.22   86-33232
ISBN 0-89680-144-6

ISBN 0-89680-144-6

To Ken, Gregory, and Eric

The *gamelan* in the *pendopo* (pavilion) could speak to you better than I. Now it is playing a lovely air . . . And my soul soars with the murmuring pure silver tones on high, on high, to the isles of blue light, to the fleecy clouds, and towards the shining stars—deep low tones are ringing now and the music leads me through dark dales, down steep ravines, through somber woods on into dense wilderness, and my soul shivers and trembles within me with anguish and pain and sorrow.

Kartini, *Letters of a Javanese Princess*

The sound carried the audience away, it was exceedingly lovely; all the listeners were fired with passion, as if driven to the most extreme erotic feelings. The power of emotion gripped the heart; the *wilet* (melodies) intoxicated the senses. As when people are united in love; so was the emotion of the heart through the gripping power of the gending, which awakened a feeling of hankering expectation, as of one looking forward, full of longing. Thus it was that the gamelan played.

Yasadipura II and Ranggasutrasna, *Serat Centhini* (translated by Jaap Kunst)

CONTENTS

PREFACE

One of the vocal styles associated with the Central Javanese orchestra, the *gamelan*, is *sindhènan*, solo female singing. In this study, I will investigate the rules of *pathet*, mode, in sindhènan. My reasons for choosing this particular area of study are three-fold.

First, very little research has been done on pathet in vocal music, even though many native Javanese scholars define pathet exclusively in vocal terms. Most studies of pathet have focused on the music of instruments found in the gamelan. The largest gongs were the subject of early pathet studies, while more recent studies (J. Becker, 1980, Templeton, 1980, McDermott and Sumarsam, 1975) have dealt with two of the metallophone types found in the gamelan, the *saron* and the *gendèr*.

Secondly, a study of *sindhènan* will illustrate very clearly the fact that different systems of pathet are in operation simultaneously in the gamelan. I will show that the system of pathet used in sindhèn melodies is very different from that used in saron melodies. In earlier research on pathet, it was assumed that if the rules for pathet of one instrument could be determined, those rules would probably apply to all the other instruments and vocal melodies of the gamelan as well. This assumption is understandable in light of the fact that Western scholars have done most of the research on pathet; in most Western music, the rules for mode, melody, and harmony apply universally to all the instruments and voices of one ensemble. In Javanese music, however, a diversity of rules within one ensemble seems to be the norm.

The study of sindhènan is particularly appropriate at this time for a third reason. This century has seen a tremendous increase of vocal music in the gamelan. Prior to about 1850, the female voice was virtually never used in a full gamelan; today, the most highly paid—as well as the most audible—musician in the gamelan is the solo female singer, the *pesindhèn*. In addition, a unison male chorus has been added to many old *gendhing* (musical pieces) as well as to gendhing composed in this century. Although this study deals only with currently popular music of the traditional style, it is interesting to note that the *kreasi baru*, compositions written in a new, unconventional style, also reflect the increasing importance of vocal music in the gamelan. What was for centuries an instrumentally dominated ensemble has been replaced by a vocally dominated one in most of the kreasi baru.

This study is not intended as a teaching manual for the student pesindhèn. Only those aspects of sindhènan germane to pathet will be examined. Both structuralist and functionalist viewpoints are considered in my examination of sindhènan and pathet. I offer an analysis of structural differences among sindhèn melodies that provides a basis for examining the function of those melodies within the gamelan: how they can be used as sole predictors of the pathet of a gendhing, and how they relate to pathet in other ways. I then compare the structures and functions of sindhèn pathet with other, instrumental, systems of pathet. Finally, I speculate on possible historical explanations for the coexistence of different systems of pathet in the gamelan.

ACKNOWLEDGMENTS

This study of mode in Javanese vocal music was originally inspired by Judith Becker's work on mode in instrumental music. I am deeply grateful to her for generously contributing many suggestions and ideas for this study. She also made available to me her private collection of unpublished books and manuscripts of musical notation which were indispensable for the musical analysis in this study.

This work also profited from research that I undertook during the year of 1974 in Java on the history of Javanese vocal music. I am indebted to LIPI (Indonesian Institute of Sciences) for sponsoring my research there.

Many Indonesians have aided me in this project. Above all, warm thanks are due to Ki Wasitodipuro with whom I have had long and illuminating conversations about the history of gamelan. In addition, as one of my first teachers of Javanese singing, he provided me with notation for many Javanese gamelan compositions. My other teachers of Javanese singing—Soepadmi Soetomo, Tukinem, and Sutarman—have also contributed greatly to my understanding of mode in vocal music. Sastrapustaka, Padmapuspita, R. L. Martopangrawit, and Hardja Susilo gave freely of their time and knowledge in discussing the historical role of sindhènan in the gamelan.

There are many others who deserve credit and thanks. I am particularly grateful to Dane Harwood, who assisted with the informational analysis and who made numerous suggestions and criticisms about other aspects of the study as well. Alicia Greene was also extremely generous in providing detailed comments on the manuscript. Stanley Hoffman,

Mode in Javanese Music

R. Anderson Sutton, Richard Wallis, and Mary Zurbuchen discussed various aspects of the paper with me. Thanks are also due to Alison Stevens Hunter for creating the cover design, to Martha Krieg for copying the Western musical notation, and to Jan Opdyke and the Center for South and Southeast Asian Studies at the University of Michigan for providing financial support and technical assistence in the production of the book. Finally, I am grateful to Kendall Walton for making many helpful suggestions on matters of content and style for this book.

MUSICAL NOTATION

For each musical example, I have used both Javanese cipher notation (*Kepatihan* notation) and a modified European staff notation. Cipher notation is read from left to right. Numbers represent pitch levels, low numbers indicating low pitch levels, and high numbers, high pitch levels. Tones are referred to as pitch levels, since each gamelan has a unique tuning: intervallic structure varies from gamelan to gamelan. Thus pitch level refers to the general position of the pitch in the scale. In practice, a pitch may be represented by many different frequencies within a limited range of frequencies. A dot below a number marks the octave lower than than the same number without a dot; a dot above a number indicates the higher octave. Thus,

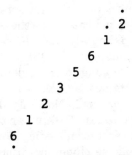

is an ascending progression in one of the two Javanese tuning systems. (This system has no pitch designated as 4.) In the text, though not in the figures, the numbers denoting pitch levels are arranged on the page to illustrate the contour of the melody. When dots appear in the notation of instruments that have only one octave, the dots are useful only as a visual clue to the melodic register of other instruments (including voice) that have multi-octave ranges. These other instruments play or sing in the range indicated by the dots, whereas the single-octave instruments cannot.

Rhythm and phrasing are notated in four ways: (1) Dots between numbers mark passage of time. In notation of vocal music, these dots do not mark specific lapses of time. In notation of instrumental music, however, these dots mark the regular passage of basic pulses. (2) Horizontal lines over numbers represent rapidly sung tones; the more horizontal lines there are, the quicker the pitches are sung. For example,

.2 3 3.5 3.2 2

would sound approximately like

(3) The vertical coincidence of numbers in the vocal and instrumental notations indicate that the specified pitches are to be sounded approximately simultaneously. (4) A line under a series of numbers (as in 3532) indicates a melisma, so that all the tones are sung to one syllable.

The musical examples are notated also in a modified version of European notation. Not only does European notation have the advantage of familiarity among Western readers, it also represents melodic shape, something not accomplished by Javanese cipher notation. Javanese pitches and intervals do not match European ones, and thus playing the musical examples on the piano will not produce Javanese melodies. The lines and spaces of the European staff are arbitrarily assigned to pitch levels of the Javanese musical system, as indicated by numbers on the staff. A horizontal brace over a series of tones in the instrumental melody indicates one four-note melodic unit called *gatra* as in

Flags and stems are to be read in the same way as in European notation. In general, the rhythm of sindhèn melodies is not precisely or consistently notated by Javanese musicians. This is because of the nonmetrical quality of sindhèn melodies and the high degree of rhythmic variability among performances of the same melody. The difficulty of translating the very imprecise Javanese rhythmic notation system into the extremely precise European system accounts for the occasional minor inconsistencies between a melody notated in cipher notation and its translation into the European system. In both cipher and European notation systems, the different kinds of gongs are labelled as follows: N = *kenong*, P = *kempul*, and G = *gong*.

ORTHOGRAPHY

The orthography for foreign terms used in this book corresponds to one of several acceptable forms currently found in Javanese publications. The "new spelling" adopted in 1972 is used, although the old spelling is retained for some personal names and bibliographic references. The principal differences between the old and new spelling systems are as follows:

Old Spelling	New Spelling	Pronounced
tj	c	*ch*in
dj	j	*j*unk
j	y	*y*es

Javanese distinguishes two kinds of *d* and two kinds of *t*. *Dh* and *th* (sometimes written *ḍ* and *ṭ*) are post-alveolar, while *d* and *t* are dental. In some Javanese publications these consonants are not differentiated, so that *pathet* would be spelled *patet*.

Various diacritics have been used by linguists to distinguish Javanese vowels. This book employs the diacritcal system found in *Javaans-Nederlands Handwoordenboek* (Pigeaud 1938).

e	lent*i*l
é	m*a*y (but without the diphthong)
è	bet

The sound â, which is pronounced *aw* as in English *law*, appears in open final syllables and in open penultimate syllables that precede open final syllables. This sound is variously spelled *a* or *o* in Javanese publications. I have used the *a*.

In this book foreign terms are italicized at their first occurrence. Titles of musical compositions are italicized while the generic names of the musical form that precede the title, eg. *ladrang*, are not italicized. Since plurality is not marked in Javanese and Indonesian, I have left plural Javanese words unmarked also: *one gamelan* and *many gamelan*.

LIST OF APPENDICES

LIST OF FIGURES

xxiv

CHAPTER 1

INTRODUCTION

A Javanese gamelan is a collection of musical instruments that are tuned together and are carved and painted in the same way. The most important instruments are made, usually, of cast bronze, but sometimes of other metals. They include suspended and pot-shaped knobbed gongs and metallophones in various sizes and shapes. There are also drums, a two-stringed bowed lute, a xylophone, a bamboo flute, a zither, and human voices. The ensembles differ in size; some consist of only a few gongs, while others have as many as fifty instruments (see pp. 2–3). The instruments are tuned differently from Western instruments, and the tuning frequently varies from one ensemble to another. For that reason, gamelan instruments of various ensembles cannot be mixed.

The presence of cast bronze instruments and knobbed gongs connect the gamelan to a broad geographical tradition of musical ensembles in Southeast Asia. There are knobbed gongs in the Philippines, Malaysia, Kampuchea, Laos, Thailand, and Burma, as well as in Indonesia. Bronze casting, which involves a complex technology, appears to have originated in Southeast Asia and then spread to China and India (Solheim 1971:330–39). The Indonesian knobbed gong ensemble, the gamelan, is found in South Sumatra, Java, Madura, Bali, Lombok, Kalimantan, and Sulawesi. My work deals with one of the most well known gamelan traditions, that of Central Java.

1

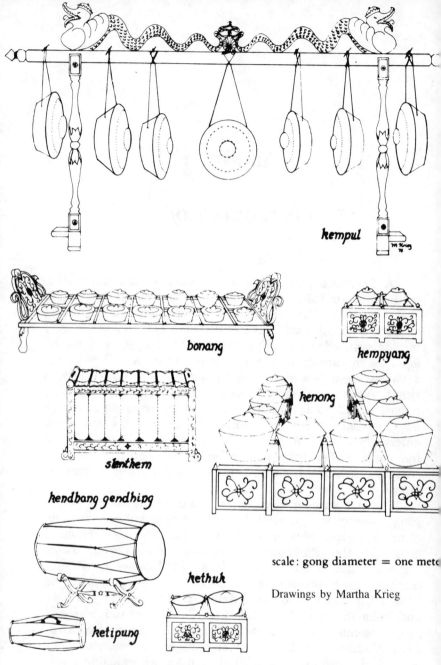

kempul

bonang

kempyang

slenthem

kenong

kendhang gendhing

scale: gong diameter = one mete[r]

Drawings by Martha Krieg

kethuk

ketipung

Figure 1. Instruments of the Javanese Gamelan

2

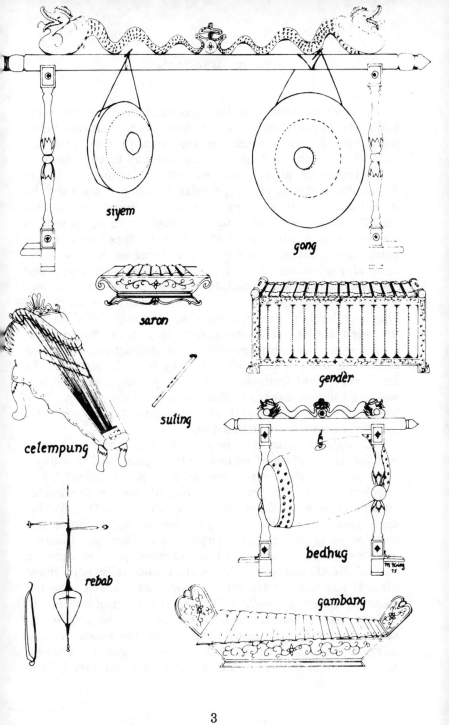

siyem

gong

saron

gendèr

celempung

suling

bedhug

rebab

gambang

3

In order to understand the gamelan, its position and function in Javanese culture must be made clear. Gamelan music constitutes a major vehicle for the culture's most profound beliefs, ideas, and feelings, and as such can be considered to be as important an art form as symphonic music is in the West. The richness of the gamelan tradition is enhanced by its intimate connection to many other art forms: drama, classical Sanskrit-based and indigenous poetry, dance, as well as the plastic arts in the form of elaborate puppet carving and batik dance costume design. The gamelan has been an integral part of Javanese life for centuries. Javanese and Balinese literature and temple carvings record the existence of some gamelan instruments in the twelfth century, and Javanese legends and histories place the origin of the tradition even earlier. In nineteenth century Java, the gamelan assumed an extremely important role in court life. Gamelan music was used in all court and state festivals, signalled the king's movement from one part of the palace to another, and was used almost daily as entertainment in the palace. Even in this century, some members of Javanese royalty regularly perform Javanese music and dance.

In addition to its importance in court life, the gamelan is popular at all levels of society, both in cities and in villages (although this situation is changing to some extent). This popularity is evident from Jaap Kunst's survey of gamelan ensembles, done in the early 1930's (1973:546–71). At that time there was a ratio of one gamelan per 2,370 people, and there were 17,282 gamelan ensembles in Java and Madura, Java's closest neighbor, which together comprise an area the size of North Carolina. Although traditionally only males played gamelan instruments, now there are all female gamelan groups as well. (With the exception of the female singers, males and females do not usually perform in the same group.) People enjoy playing gamelan music in small informal groups. The music is not considered esoteric, abstruse, or in any way inaccessible to the ordinary person.

4

Almost identical repertoire, musical treatment, and stylistic features can be found in courts, cities, and villages.

The genuine popularity at all levels of society of an art tradition associated with the aristocracy and the highest forms of art is surprising by Western standards. One reason for this popularity is the gamelan's association with rituals and festivals in which every Javanese participates. Not only birth, puberty, marriage, and national holidays, but also house building, exorcising evil spirits, and celebrations of many other kinds are occasions for dramatic performances in which the gamelan plays a major part.

Frequently, these dramatic performances are in the form of *wayang kulit*, or shadow puppet plays, which last all night. The gamelan is played almost continuously throughout the night, though fresh musicians often relieve the tired ones at the midpoint of the performance. The intricate carving and painting of the puppets, the profound moral, religious, and philosophical content of the stories, the clowns' antics and humorous comments on current events, and the beauty of the music combine to form both a deep expression of Javanese values and a very enjoyable form of entertainment. Indeed, entertainment and ritual are not as clearly separated in Javanese culture as in our own.

Gamelan music played even outside of ritual contexts often has a spiritual element. When a shadow play is performed, the Javanese say that everyone within earshot is safe from evil spirits and is spiritually blessed. Listening to or performing gamelan music evokes in the Javanese a feeling of safety from evil and a sense of balance with the world. This is not to say that gamelan music is not considered passionate by the Javanese. On the contrary, as the two epigraphs (see p. vii) reveal, gamelan music evokes strong emotional responses in the Javanese. However, through gamelan music and the other arts as well, the Javanese are permitted to experience fully emotions of which the etiquette of Javanese life does not allow verbal or active expression. Restraint of the emotions, a sense of balance, and showing a calm exterior are important Javanese cultural values. For this reason, Javanese occasionally play on a single gamelan instrument as a form of discipline or meditation.

The value that the Javanese place on calmness and balance is reflected in the virtually perfect balance of instruments in the gamelan ensemble. At least traditionally, no one instrument is allowed to dominate. Playing gamelan music is not considered an occasion for a display of virtuosity, nor for individual artistic expression. For this reason, fine musicians are usually not acclaimed nor given celebrity status as they are in the West, although this situation is changing with respect to the *pesindhèn*, the solo female singer.

The balance of instruments in the gamelan ensemble is achieved musically through the simultaneous interplay of many different musical lines. I do not believe that there is one underlying melody upon which the other instruments' melodies are based, although this point is controversial. It is tempting to assign this role to the *saron*, a middle ranged metallophone, because the saron melody was the only line chosen to be notated when, due to Western influence, a notation system was developed.[1] However, studies done by Sutton (1975:189–207) and Sumarsam (1975 and 1984) suggest that the saron melody not only does not usually occupy this central position, but also that it is less important than several other instruments in expressing the main melodic content of a piece.

How are the polyphonic lines related, if they are not variations on some underlying melody? According to Sutton and Sumarsam, the polyphonic lines *are* all based on an underlying melody, but one that is never stated literally or fully sounded. This melody exists in complete form only in the minds of the musicians, and they frequently have somewhat different concepts of it. This underlying melody is called *lagu* in Javanese, and Sumarsam refers to it as "inner melody." Each instrument sounds a different variant of this

6

inner melody. According to Sutton's main informant, the major burden of expressing this inner melody is carried by the following instruments, listed in order of importance: *rebab* (bowed lute), *gambang* (xylophone), *gendèr* (metallophone), *gérong* (male chorus) and pesindhèn.

All the instruments of the gamelan express the inner melody by means of melodic formulas, or short melodic units. These melodies are called formulas because they or variations on them occur whenever a given kind of inner melody occurs. Similar melodic formulas occur in many pieces since portions of the inner melody of one piece are frequently like portions of the inner melody of another. These formulas are idiomatic for each instrument, since each instrument or instrument type has a distinct playing style, tonal quality, and octave range. For example, for a certain type of inner melody, the gambang might play one melodic formula, while the gendèr would play another. Melodic formulas are not rigidly fixed but are constantly being altered so that new formulas are created. Even in a piece with many repetitious portions a musician seldom repeats his melodic formulas exactly.

The different variants on the inner melody, expressed through melodic formulas, are sounded simultaneously or almost simultaneously by all the instruments of the gamelan. This brings us to the question of how the musicians know, in the absence of notation, when to move on to the next section of the inner melody and what the next section will be. A Javanese musician usually knows a large repertoire of pieces from memory. But if his memory slips, the statements of the other instruments will immediately indicate to him what the inner melody is, for he knows the kinds of melodic formulas allowable for all the instruments of the gamelan. Furthermore, some of the formulas are predictive: they indicate what the inner melody will be in the next few beats or section. For most instruments a musician needs more information about the next section (or he needs it sooner) than that provided by these predictive formulas. However, for a few instruments and notably the female vocal

7

part, a musician can frequently play or sing an entire piece he or she has never heard before just by listening to the other instruments.

The rhythmic structure of gamelan pieces also helps musicians know when to move on to the next musical idea. The pieces are all cyclical. The cycles vary in length, either 8, 16, 32, 64, 128, or 256 beats. The end point of the cycle is marked by a stroke on the largest gong and intermediate points are marked by strokes on the smaller hanging gongs *(kempul)* or the pot gongs *(kenong, kethuk,* and *kempyang).* The regular beats that make up a cycle are defined in various complex ways by the relationship of the *bonang* (a set of pot gongs) and saron and are usually played on the saron. Since the inner melody is frequently divided into four beat segments, the musicians can predict exactly when to go on to the next segment of the inner melody. The gongs segment the piece into short sections of even lengths enabling the musicians to conceptualize it easily.

In sum, gamelan music has a high degree of predictability. The same melodic formulas appear in many pieces. The segments of the inner melody are strung together in a logical and often predictable fashion; some of the formulas themselves are predictive. For all these reasons, there is not as much need for notation as there is in Western music and until recently notation was never used. The melodic formulas are passed on orally. A notation system has been developed, however, but usually only the saron and gong lines are notated. Until recently, the notation was used only as a device for preserving pieces, not as an aid for learning new ones.

I have been describing gamelan music as it is in its traditional setting. This picture is still largely accurate for Java today. However, both the role of gamelan music in Javanese culture and the music itself are changing (Becker 1980). Although gamelan music has traditionally been played in ritual settings, it is now used increasingly purely as entertainment. Perhaps this is related to the increasing popularity among Javanese youth of both Western and Indonesian popular music, which compete with the traditional forms. Whether due to the greater emphasis on entertainment, Western influence, or other reasons, gamelan music is becoming more and more dominated by a single "instrument," the solo female voice of the pesindhèn. On recordings of gamelan music made only fifty years ago the pesindhèn is frequently barely audible, while on contemporary recordings it is sometimes difficult to hear the instruments of the gamelan because of the pesindhèn's dominance. The music that the pesindhèn sings, however, is for the most part traditional.

This book describes one of the most traditional and fundamental aspects of gamelan music—mode—as it relates to the instrument in the gamelan whose role has changed most in recent times: the female voice.

CHAPTER 2

SINDHÈNAN IN THE GAMELAN

SINDHÈN CÈNGKOK

The pesindhèn sings either alone or simultaneously with a unison male chorus, called *gérong*, whose melody contrasts with the melody of the pesindhèn. The word "sindhèn" is sometimes used as a generic term for singing, as in *sindhèn bedhaya*, a unison chorus of male and female voices. In this study, however, "sindhèn" will refer only to the music of the solo female singer.

Despite the increasing prominence of the sindhèn melody in the gamelan, the pesindhèn does not usually play the leading musical role in the gamelan in the way that a vocal soloist in European music usually does. Whereas the vocal parts of European music are usually indispensable, this is generally not true of the vocal parts of Javanese gendhing. Those gendhing types in which the sindhèn melody is indispensable—*dolanan* and *jineman*—represent a minor part of the repertoire. Instead of functioning as a leader, the pesindhèn is valued for providing an additional and different tone color to the music, just as the tone color of the gambang, a wooden xylophone, contrasts with that of the gendèr, a metallophone with tube resonators.

With few exceptions, the pesindhèn does not sing a melody that is associated exclusively with a specific piece. Instead, she sings melodic formulas, or *cèngkok*, which are common to many different gendhing. The beginnings and

11

endings of cèngkok are easily perceptible as there are usually pauses between cèngkok. Figure 2 illustrates two different sindhèn cèngkok or formulas written both in Javanese and in modified European notation.

Figure 2. Two Cèngkok from Gendhing *Gambir Sawit*, Sléndro Pathet Sanga (Sindhèn Cèngkok Notated by Ki Wasitodipuro)

Cèngkok 1:

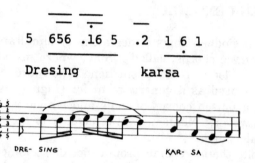

Cèngkok 2:

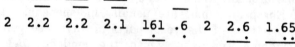

12

Sindhèn cèngkok are related to the final note of four-beat melodic patterns played on the saron. These four-beat patterns are called *gatra*. Two examples are:

$$. . 3 \overset{\bullet}{5} \quad \text{and} \quad 6 . 1 \overset{\bullet}{6}$$

The dots (indicating rests) and the numbers (indicating pitch levels) are played as four even pulses. Figure 3 illustrates the relationship of saron gatra to sindhèn cèngkok.

Figure 3.   An Excerpt from Ketawang *Suksma Ilang*, Sléndro Pathet Manyura (Sindhèn Cèngkok Sung by Tukinem)

sar   .   .   3   5   6   .   i̇   6N

pes   2̇ 3̇ 2̇ 1̇2̈/ 6 5 36 6

N=keNong sar=saron pes=pesindhèn

The pesindhèn sings a cèngkok whose last pitch level is the same as the last pitch level of the gatra being played on the saron.[1] Most pesindhèn, however, do not conclude their cèngkok until after the last pitch level of the saron gatra has been sounded. In Figure 3, the last pitch level of the sindhèn cèngkok (pitch level 6) matches the last pitch level of the second saron gatra. This cèngkok is called a 6 cèngkok since it ends on pitch level 6. The justification for labelling cèngkok according to their last pitch level is two-fold: (1) The last pitch level of the cèngkok is the most important for it is the only pitch level in the cèngkok that has to match any particular pitch level played on the saron, as explained above. (2) Javanese music theorists classify sindhèn cèngkok on the basis of the last pitch level of the cèngkok (Gitosaprodjo, no date a:1–4).

Figure 4.   Excerpt from Ladrang *Wilujeng*, Sléndro
Pathet Manyura (Sindhèn Cèngkok Notated
by Gitosaprodjo)

As mentioned earlier, cèngkok are common to many different gendhing. The cèngkok in Tukinem's version of Ketawang *Suksma Ilang* (Figure 3) are also heard in many other gendhing. The 6 cèngkok in Figure 3 is also heard in

Gitosaprodjo's version of Ladrang *Wilujeng*, sléndro pathet manyura (Figure 4.)

The 6 cèngkok notated in Ketawang *Suksma Ilang* (Figure 3) is not the only 6 cèngkok that is allowable in that particular place. The pesindhèn can choose from a great variety of 6 cèngkok or formulas ending on pitch level 6. Ki Wasitodipuro's cèngkok for Ketawang *Suksma Ilang* (Figure 5) is quite different from Tukinem's cèngkok (Figure 3). Figures 3, 4, and 5 illustrate that sindhènan employs a repertoire of melodic formulas, from which the pesindhèn can choose.

Figure 5. An Excerpt from Ketawang *Suksma Ilang*, Sléndro Pathet Manyura (Sindhèn Cèngkok Notated by Ki Wasitodipuro)

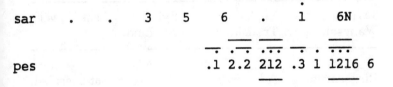

SINDHÈN TEXTS

Just as the pesindhèn can choose from a variety of cèngkok for any given piece, she can also choose from a variety of poetic texts for any piece. When singing together, the pesindhèn and gérong may use any poem of a particular genre.[2] Gendhing structure and gendhing length determine the choice of poetic genre. Poetic genres are distinguished by the number of poetic lines, the number of syllables per line, and the final vowel of each line.

When singing without the gérong, the pesindhèn usually sings a poem of the genre called *wangsalan*. The formal features of this poetic genre are illustrated in Figure 6.

Figure 6. A Wangsalan

Javanese Wangsalan	English Translation	Syllables per Line	Last Vowel
Riris harda	A heavy rain	4	not specified
Hardané wong lumaksana	A great many people are walking about	8	a
Dresing karsa	Many plans	4	not specified
Mamayu-hayu ning praja	To accomplish much for the country.	8	a

Sindhènan in the Gamelan

Pigeaud (1967:260) defines the wangsalan as a poetic form of two lines of twelve syllables each. Because each twelve syllable unit is almost always divided into four and eight syllable units in sindhèn performance, in this study I refer to the wangsalan as a four line poetic form. Although the major syntactic division of the wangsalan is at the half-way point, further subdivision of the two halves does not disrupt the syntax or result in word splitting.

In all wangsalan, an enigma or riddle in the form of a phrase or word (often referring to nature) in the first half of the poem is solved by a phrase or word in the second half that suggests, by assonance or synonymity, the first phrase or word. For example, a synonym for "heavy rain" in the first line of the wangsalan quoted above is *deres*, which sounds the same as the first syllable of the word *dresing* in the third line of the wangsalan.

Usually, the four lines of the wangsalan are sung at the four main subdivisions of the gendhing: the end, the half point, and the two quarter points. These subdivisions often coincide with strokes on the largest gongs of the gamelan: the *gong ageng* (largest gong in the ensemble, usually called "gong"), the kenong and sometimes, the kempul.

The location of poetic lines at important structural points in a gendhing is related to a Javanese theory about weak and strong beats in saron gatra. According to Gitosaprodjo (1971a:5 and in press) every saron gatra is subdivided into two parts, *dhing*, or weak stress, and *dhong*, or strong stress as follows:

Each unit is further subdivided in like manner, as follows:

17

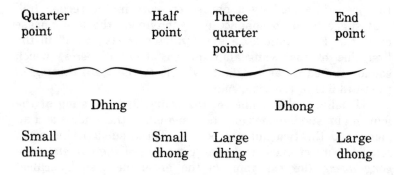

1   2   3   2

Small dhing   Small dhong   Large dhing   Large dhong

The same concept of weak and strong stress can be applied to all musical units in gamelan, including gendhing structure. The dhing and dhong units of a gendhing might be diagramed as follows:

Quarter point	Half point	Three quarter point	End point

Dhing   Dhong

| Small dhing | | Small dhong | Large dhing | | Large dhong |

The location of the four lines of a wangsalan in the gendhing structure reinforces this alternation of dhing and dhong: The long lines, of eight syllables, occur at the half and end points, while the short lines, of four syllables, usually coincide with the quarter points, at small dhing and large dhing. Frequently the pesindhèn emphasizes the large dhong even more by combining the second two lines of the wangsalan to make a twelve syllable line that is sung as one cèngkok at the end of a section.

For further subdivisions of the gendhing (at the 8th, 16th, 32nd, 64th, etc. points of subdivision), the pesindhèn usually sings non-obligatory semi-nonsense "fillers," called *isèn-isèn*. The isèn-isèn words have no textual relationship to the wangsalan. The following are examples of typical isèn-isèn:

mas	term of direct address used to a young man
bapak	term of direct address used to an older male
gonas ganès	coquettish
éman-éman	regrettable; related forms mean to care for deeply, to cherish

Some of the sindhèn texts have a flirtatious or even erotic element. The translation of the isèn-isèn above suggests this, for in a society in which males and females do not associate freely, even a direct address from a female to a male could be considered flirtatious. This hint at eroticism is enhanced by the presence in the gamelan of the pesindhèn, for the pesindhèn is the direct descendent of the *talèdhèk*, street singer, dancer and sometimes prostitute. Also, the pesindhèn are the only females in an otherwise exclusively male group. The erotic element in the texts corresponds to the emotional environment created by gamelan music as the *Centhini* quotation in the epigraph suggests.

The relationship of poetic texts and cèngkok is interesting for several reasons. Usually, the same cèngkok are used for all types of poetic texts; whether wangsalan, isèn-isèn, or poems sung with the gérong. Secondly, within a single cèngkok, there is seldom a one-to-one relationship between the notes of the cèngkok and the words of the poem; instead, melismas are the rule. However, cèngkok and poetic lines correspond: usually one cèngkok employs one line of poetry (see the first cèngkok in Figure 2). Occasionally, however, the first two or the last two lines of a wangsalan are sung together as one cèngkok (see the second cèngkok in Figure 2).

SINDHÈN PATHET

In the discussion of sindhèn cèngkok, I indicated that the pesindhèn can choose from a repertoire of cèngkok. However, her choices are not entirely free, but rather are limited by several factors. The most important factor is *pathet*, or mode. There are three different pathet in each of two tuning systems in a complete gamelan. One tuning system, known as *laras sléndro*, has five pitch levels per octave, labelled 1, 2, 3, 5, 6 in ascending order. The other tuning system, *laras pélog*, has seven pitch levels: 1, 2, 3, 4, 5, 6, and 7. The three pathet in each laras are:

Laras Sléndro	Laras Pélog
pathet nem	pathet lima
pathet sanga	pathet nem
pathet manyura	pathet barang

The similarity of the two 6 cèngkok in Ketawang *Suksma Ilang* (Figure 3, p.13) and Ladrang *Wilujeng* (Figure 4, p.14) can be explained by the fact that both pieces are in the same pathet, sléndro pathet manyura. Likewise, the differences between the two 2 cèngkok in Figure 7 can be attributed to the different pathet of the two cèngkok: the first cèngkok is in pathet sanga, while the second is in pathet manyura.

In this study, I will examine only the three sléndro pathet. Pélog pathet determination is relatively simple due to the almost exclusive use of some pitch levels in some pathet. The next chapter will focus on the differences among sindhèn cèngkok of the three sléndro pathet.

Figure 7. Two 2 Cèngkok

Cèngkok 1, from Ladrang *Éling-éling Kasmaran*, Sléndro Pathet Sanga (Sindhèn Cèngkok Notated by Ki Wasitodipuro):

$$\overline{.3} \quad 5 \quad \overline{53} \; \overline{565} \; \overline{3.2}$$

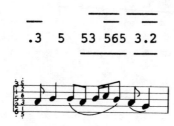

Cèngkok 2, from Ketawang *Suksma Ilang*, Sléndro Pathet Manyura (Sindhèn Cèngkok Notated by Ki Wasitodipuro):

$$\overline{.2} \quad 3 \quad \overline{3 \; .5} \; \overline{3 \; .2} \quad 2$$

CHAPTER 3

THE RELATIONSHIP
OF THE THREE SLÉNDRO PATHET

This chapter is concerned with how pathet functions in sléndro sindhèn cèngkok. After introducing the data base, I will suggest two principles of sindhèn pathet. The first one, which concerns pathet manyura and pathet sanga, governs (1) the construction of long cèngkok, short cèngkok, *plèsèdan* cèngkok, and non-plèsèdan cèngkok of three patterns and (2) the relationship of the various segments of a sindhèn cèngkok. The second principle of pathet explains sindhèn cèngkok in pathet nem gendhing.

THE DATA BASE

The data for this study consist of twelve gendhing in pathet manyura, ten gendhing in pathet sanga, and eight gendhing in pathet nem. The saron and sindhèn melodies for all these gendhing are notated in Appendices 2, 3, 4, and 5. These gendhing provide a representative sampling of Central Javanese sindhèn styles. Most of the gendhing are taken from three sources: (1) notation by Ki Wasitodipuro, composer and for many years musical director of the Paku Alaman Court in Yogyakarta, (2) my own transcriptions of field recordings of Tukinem, a pesindhèn at the Radio

Republik Indonesia Gamelan at Surakarta, and (3) notation of Sulaiman Gitosaprodjo, a music theorist who studied at the Konservatori Karawitan Indonesia in Surakarta (Gitosaprodjo, no date b). There are a few gendhing from other sources: notation of Kenang Darmoredjono from Wonogiri, notation of Prawotosaputro from Surakarta, my own transcription of parts of a wayang kulit in which Soetrisno of Surakarta was the *dhalang* (puppeteer), and my own transcription of gendhing sung by Ngabéhi Mardusari and by Soepadmi Soetomo.

As noted above, some of these gendhing are taken from written sources (the notation provided by Javanese musicians), while others are taken from aural sources (my own transcriptions of recordings of gendhing). There is no major disparity, however, between these two kinds of sources. The written sources in no way represent a theoretical sindhènan that is different from the actual practice of sindhènan. Many of the cèngkok appearing in the written sources can be heard in the aural sources, as Figure 8 illustrates. In Figure 8, the initial parts of fifteen cèngkok in pathet manyura and pathet sanga are listed. For purposes of analysis which I will discuss presently, I have divided most cèngkok into two parts called initial patterns and final patterns. These fifteen initial patterns represent all of the initial patterns of a certain type (labelled 1.1) found in the data. The sources of the initial patterns are also noted.

PRINCIPLES OF PATHET FOR SINDHÈN CÈNGKOK

Almost all sindhèn cèngkok are associated exclusively with either pathet manyura or pathet sanga. In my data, which consist of approximately 140 different cèngkok in pathet sanga and approximately 115 different cèngkok in pathet manyura, cèngkok used in pathet manyura gendhing are, with only one exception, the cèngkok

Figure 8.   Similarity of the Different Sources

Pathet Manyura Patterns	Source(s)
.. 61263216123 .	Tukinem(a)
... 61216(3)	R.Soetrisno(a) Gitosaprodjo(w) Ki Wasitodipuro(w)
..... 6121216(3)	Ki Wasitodipuro(w)
.... 612126	Ki Wasitodipuro(w)
.. 6(r)12(6[3])	R. Soetrisno(a) Gitosaprodjo(w) Ki Wasitodipuro(w)
.. 5612	Tukinem(a) Ki Wasitodipuro(w)
.. 12r63	R. Soetrisno(a)

Figure 8 (continued)

Pathet Sanga Patterns	Source(s)
5̇615215612̈	Ki Wasitodipuro(w)
561̇r52532	Prawotosaputro(w)
561̇(r)65	Ki Wasitodipuro(w) Gitosaprodjo(w)
561̇(r)5	Gitosaprodjo(w)
5̇6162̈165	Ki Wasitodipuro(w)
5(r)61̇(52)	Tukinem(a) Ki Wasitodipuro(w)
3r561̇5r	Gitosaprodjo(w)
561̇65	Ki Wasitodipuro(w)

w = written source a = aural source

$$612 \text{ or } \overset{..}{6}1\underset{.}{2}$$

never heard in pathet sanga gendhing.

The distinctiveness of pathet manyura and pathet sanga cèngkok and their relationship to pathet nem cèngkok can be expressed as two basic principles of sindhèn pathet:

Principle I. The sindhèn cèngkok in pathet sanga gendhing are lowered one pitch level from the cèngkok used in pathet manyura gendhing.

For example, a pathet manyura 2 cèngkok such as

$$\begin{array}{ccc} 2 & & 2 \\ & 1 \quad 1 & \\ & \underset{.}{6} & \end{array}$$

becomes the pathet sanga 1 cèngkok

$$\begin{array}{ccc} 1 & & 1 \\ & \underset{.}{6} \quad \underset{.}{6} & \\ & \underset{.}{5} & \end{array}$$

These two cèngkok are said to have the same *contour*, the same pattern of ascending and descending pitch levels. The question might be asked: what evidence is there that pathet manyura is the parent pathet from which pathet sanga cèngkok are derived, rather than the reverse? Both analyses are equally rational, given the relationship of the two cèngkok above. The primacy of pathet manyura is supported by the following statement of Gitosaprodjo:

Important: Cèngkok sléndro sanga = cèngkok sléndro manyura lowered one note (Gitosapradjo, no date a:2).[1]

27

Mode in Javanese Music

Furthermore he refers to pathet manyura cèngkok as *wilet dasar*, or "basic melodies" (1970a:13). Speculations about why pathet manyura can be considered the "basic" pathet for sindhènan will be discussed later.

Principle II. Gendhing in pathet nem are primarily composed of sindhèn cèngkok of both pathet manyura and pathet sanga. In addition, there are a few sindhèn cèngkok used exclusively in pathet nem.

I owe the main outlines of this hypothesis to Gitosaprodjo and to his teachers, R. L. Martopangrawit, Sutarman, and S. Tjiptasuwarsa. Gitosaprodjo not only clearly articulates the relationship of pathet manyura and pathet sanga cèngkok as quoted above, but he also lists twenty-five pathet manyura sindhèn cèngkok followed by the corresponding pathet sanga cèngkok, lowered one pitch level from the pathet manyura cèngkok. In support of the second principle, he lists no cèngkok for pathet nem, and he states:

In practice, the cèngkok or melodies for sléndro pathet nem are a combination of cèngkok of pathet sanga and pathet manyura (1971a:6 and in press).[2]

PRINCIPLE I IN FOUR KINDS OF CÈNGKOK

In order to illustrate how the two pathet principles operate, I have classified sindhèn cèngkok into four categories: (1) long cèngkok, (2) short cèngkok, (3) plèsèdan cèngkok, and (4) non-plèsèdan cèngkok of three patterns. Differentiation of the four cèngkok types is a function of the number and kinds of segments constituting the cèngkok. In this study, the word *cèngkok* will refer to a complete melodic unit, and the word *pattern* will refer to a segment of a cèngkok. Cèngkok may consist of one to three patterns. I will explain shortly how I propose to divide cèngkok into patterns.

Figure 9. Long Initial Patterns in Sléndro Pathet Manyura and Sléndro Pathet Sanga

Manyura	Sanga

```
                C   A   T   E   G   O   R   Y   1 . 1

          ..                                .
  6       12        63216123          5     61          5215612
                         .                                    ..
                                      5     61r         52 5 32
          ..    .                           .
  6       12    16    (3)             5     61(r)    6 5
                                            .
                                      5     61(r)    5
          .. ..  .
  6       12 12 16    (3)                   .    ..
                                      5     61 6 21 6 5
          .. ..
  6       12 12 6
                                            .
          ..                                .
  6(r)    12      (6   [3])           5(r)  61        (5      2)
          ..                                .
 56       12                          3r5   61        5r
                                            .
          ..                                .
 12r      6     3                     565   61 6      5

                C   A   T   E   G   O   R   Y   1 . 2

   .   .. ..
 6r2   12 12  6r
                                       .    .
                                      5r1   61        5
   .   ..                              .    .
 6r2   12    6r                       5r1   61        5r
                                       .             .
                                      5r1   6 5 6 1(6)5
   .                                   .
 6     2    6                         5r    1         5      2

                C   A   T   E   G   O   R   Y   1 . 3

  .       . ..                              .   .
 616     2(12) 6     (3)               565  1  6(1)  5     2
  .       . ..
 616     2 12  63   353
                                            .
                                       565  1        5     2
  .       . ..
 616     2 12  6r
```

29

Figure 9 (continued)

```
          Manyura                    Sanga

              C A T E G O R Y   2 . 1

 . .     . .  .                .           .
 2 3     2 1  2(6[3])      1   2   1   6   1(5[2])
 . .     .... .
 2 3     2121 2 6 3
                          .. .  .   .       .
                          12 1  2   1   6   1 5 2
 . .     ..   ..          .     .   .       .
 2 3r    21   612 6 3     1     2   1   65r61 5 2
                          .     .   .       .
                          1     2r  1   65 61 5

 2 3     2 1
                          .     .   .       .
                          61    2   1   6   1 5 2
                          .     .
                          1     2               5
   3     2 1 2            .     .   .       .
                                2r  1   6   1 5 2

              C A T E G O R Y   2 . 2

 . .     .   . .
 2 3r    1   2 6 3        (1)   2       6   1 5 2

 2 3     1   2(6)
 . .     .   . .
 2 3     1   2(6 3)       .(r)  2       6   1
                          1
                          .     .       6   1 532
                          1     2
 . .     ... ..           .     .   .       .
 2 3     121 216          1     2 (61) 6   165
                          .     . . .
... .    ...              1     2 61 616     5
12 3r    121    6
 . .     . .
 2 3r    1 2
 . .     . .
 2r3     1 2

              C A T E G O R Y   2 . 3

 . . ...  . .             .     . ...      .
 2 3 532  1 2             1     2 321  6 1(5[2])
                                        .
 2   532        6         .     . ..
                          1     2 32
 2 3r532
```

30

Figure 9 (continued)

Manyura   Sanga

```
      C  A  T  E  G  O  R  Y    3  .  1

3(r)2r(12)1   3        2r1r(61)    6           2
                         .   .       .          .
                       2r1r  61(r)  6          2

3r          1   3

3r    2r    3   1

6r    5r    3   6      5r3r(23)    2           5

      C  A  T  E  G  O  R  Y    3  .  2

3r    2r    16123      2r1r       6 1 6 5612
.     .        ...      .          .  . ..
1     2r       6123    6 1r       6(1r6)5612

      C  A  T  E  G  O  R  Y    3  .  3

3r    56 3

3     5653             23532
      .
      1r653
```

Key:
   r = repeated
   (x) = x is optional
   (x[y]) = xy and y are optional

Long Cèngkok

Cèngkok that consist of a long initial pattern and a final pattern are called *long cèngkok*. They are usually used for poetic lines of eight to twelve syllables. The cèngkok

```
   3 3         3 /   3
      2 2              2
         1      1    1
                       6
                       .
```

is an example of a long cèngkok. The diagonal line marks the division between the initial and final patterns. The same initial pattern appears with other final patterns as in

```
                  5
    3 3       3 /  3 3
       2 2            2 2
          1
```

and the same final pattern appears with other initial patterns as in

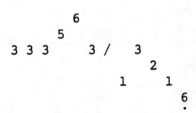

The repeatability of a portion of a cèngkok provides the main justification for segmenting the cèngkok into patterns. Textual considerations play only a minor role in determining the division between initial and final patterns, and division of the cèngkok in the middle of a word occurs only rarely in my analysis. When it is difficult to determine where the dividing line between the initial and final pattern of a cèngkok should be placed, the manner in which the cèngkok is phrased indicates the proper point of division.[3]

Figure 9 (pp. 29–31) illustrates how the first principle of sindhèn pathet is manifested in long sindhèn cèngkok. This figure lists all of the long initial patterns found in all the pathet manyura and pathet sanga gendhing in Appendices 2–3.[4] Patterns are lined up vertically so that the similarities of pitch usage in each category are clearly apparent. Spaces between numbers in a given pattern do not mark rhythm, but merely allow space for numbers present in other patterns. There are four major categories of initial patterns of cèngkok, labelled 1, 2, 3, and 4 for pathet manyura and pathet sanga. Categories 1–3 are further subdivided to show minor differences in contour and pitch usage. The distinctions among the four major categories within each pathet are contour, not pitch. For example, the predominant contour of category 1 can be represented graphically as

whereas the predominant contour of category 2 has a different contour:

The significant fact illustrated by Figure 9 is that the pathet manyura patterns have almost exact counterparts in pathet sanga, lowered one pitch level, which is the first principle of sindhèn pathet. For example, the first pathet manyura pattern in category 1.1 is

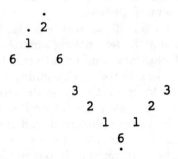

The corresponding pathet sanga pattern,

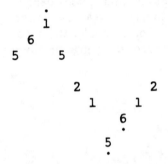

is an almost exact copy of the pathet manyura patterns lowered one pitch level.

Each contour in Figure 9 is realized on only one pitch level (except for contour 3.1, which is realized on two pitch levels in each pathet). This means that all the patterns listed on the pathet manyura side of Figure 9 are used exclusively in pathet manyura, and all the patterns on the pathet sanga side are used exclusively in pathet sanga. For example, the pathet manyura pattern in category 3.1

```
        6r        6
          5r
            3
```

is never heard in gendhing in pathet sanga. (The letter "r" indicates a repeated pitch level.)

The only apparent exception to the exclusive use of a pattern in either pathet manyura or pathet sanga is the pathet manyura pattern

```
              5
         3r      3
      2             2
```

in category 2.3 and the pathet sanga pattern

```
              5
          3      3
       2           2
```

in category 4.1. These two patterns, however, are sung quite differently, for the pitch level 5 in the pathet manyura pattern functions as an upper neighbor trill tone to more important surrounding pitches, whereas the pitch level 5 in the pathet sanga pattern is stressed rhythmically, as illustrated in Figure 10 (p. 36).

Like the initial patterns in Figure 9, most pathet manyura final patterns appear in pathet sanga, lowered one pitch level. All of the final patterns found in the pathet manyura and pathet sanga gendhing in Appendices 2–3 are listed in Figure 11 (pp. 37–42). The different types of final patterns are labelled alphabetically (Aa, Ab, Ac, etc.) in contrast to the numerical labelling of the initial patterns (1.1, 1.2, etc.).

Figure 10. Two Similar Patterns in Sléndro Pathet
Manyura and Sléndro Pathet Sanga

Cèngkok 1 from *Srepegan*, Sléndro Pathet Manyura:

$$2 \quad 3 \quad \overline{3532} \ / \ \overline{32} \ 1$$

Ra- dèn ra - dèn

Cèngkok 2 from Ladrang *Clunthang*, Sléndro Pathet Sanga:

$$2 \quad 3 \quad 5 \quad 3 \quad 2/ \ 2 \ \overline{32} \ 1 \ \overset{\cdot}{6}$$

-man é - man é - man é - man

Figure 11. Final Patterns in Sléndro Pathet Manyura and Sléndro Pathet Sanga

Manyura   Sanga

```
        C   A   T   E   G   O   R   Y     Aa

        6(r)5  3  6r                5  3  2  5r

                                         2r5r

                                    2  3  2  5
```

```
        C   A   T   E   G   O   R   Y     Ba
                  .
         3  5  6  1r                2  3  5  6(r)
                  .
        5  3  5  6  1              3  2  3  5  6
                  .
     6r5  3  5  6  1
                  .
     (6)  3  5  6  1
                  .
         6  1  2  3r        5  6      1      2r
         .                  .  .
      (1)6  1  2  3       6  5  6      1      2
         .                .  .  .
                         5  6 1 6 1 2 3 2
                         .  .     .
      2  6  1  2  3
         .
     5  3  2  3  5  6          3  2  1  2  3  5
```

```
        C   A   T   E   G   O   R   Y     Bb

        1  6  1  2              (1)6  5  6  1
           .                       .  .  .
                                            .
                               (5)6  5  6  1

                                  3  2  1  2  3
```

37

Figure 11 (continued)

```
        Manyura          Sanga

  ┌─────────────────────────────────┐
  │ C   A   T   E   G   O   R   Y  Bc│
  │              .                   │
  │ 5 6 3 1        (5)3 5 2 6         │
  ├─────────────────────────────────┤
  │ C   A   T   E   G   O   R   Y  Bd│
  │                                  │
  │     6 2              5r1r        │
  │       .                          │
  │                 1 6 1 5 1(r)     │
  │                   .   .          │
  ├─────────────────────────────────┤
  │ C   A   T   E   G   O   R   Y  Be│
  │            .                     │
  │   5 6 1(r)          3 5 6        │
  │   . .                      .     │
  │ 6(r)1 2             5r6 1        │
  │   . .                      .     │
  │ 6   1 2r            5r6 1r       │
  │                            .     │
  │                   5 6 5 6 1      │
  │                     . .          │
  │ (2)1 2 3            6 1 2        │
  │                                  │
  │                     6 1 2        │
  │                       .          │
  │                   1 6 1 2r       │
  │                     .            │
  ├─────────────────────────────────┤
  │ C   A   T   E   G   O   R   Y  Bf│
  │                            .     │
  │     1 2(r)          6 1          │
  │                                  │
  │     2 3             1 2          │
  └─────────────────────────────────┘
```

Figure 11 (continued)

```
         Manyura                    Sanga

┌─────────────────────────────┬──────────────────────────┐
│     C  A  T  E  G  O  R  Y   Ca                         │
│                                                         │
│        3 1(r)2 1 6               2 6 1 6 5              │
│              .                     .     . .            │
│        . .    . .                  .   .                │
│        3 1   2 1 6               2 6 1 6 5              │
├─────────────────────────────┼──────────────────────────┤
│     C  A  T  E  G  O  R  Y   Cb                         │
│                                                         │
│        3 6r5 3     2             2 5(r)3 2 1            │
│        3 6r5 3 5 3 2                                    │
│        3 6(5)3     2                                    │
│     5r3 6   3      2r                                   │
│     3 5 3 6r5 3    2             2 3 2 5r  3 2 1        │
│  ([5]3)5 3 6 5 3   2                                    │
│        (3)1 3 2 1 6            2 6 2      1 6 5          │
│                  .              .          . .          │
│                               6 2(1 6)  1 6 5          │
│                               .      .    . .           │
├─────────────────────────────┼──────────────────────────┤
│     C  A  T  E  G  O  R  Y   Cc                         │
│                                                         │
│        5 3 2r1            (3 2[3 2])3 2 1 6            │
│                                          .              │
│                                   3 2 1 6r              │
│                                        .                │
│        6 5 3 2                    5 3 2 1               │
│        .                                                │
│        1 6 5 3                  6 5 3 2(r)              │
│        1 6 5 3                                          │
│        . . .                                            │
│        3 2 1 6                                          │
│              .                                          │
└─────────────────────────────┴──────────────────────────┘
```

39

Figure 11 (continued)

```
          Manyura                Sanga

        C  A  T  E  G  O  R  Y    Cd

        3 5 3 2 1                 2 3 2(1 6)1 6
                                       .      .
                                 2 3 2 3 2    1 6
                                              .
          .
        6 1 6 5(r)3             (5 3)5 6 5 3      2
          .
        6r1 6 5    3

                                   5 6 5(3 2)3 2

          .
        6 1   5   3r
        . . .
        1 2 1 6   5r

                                 3 5 3 2 3 2 1


        C  A  T  E  G  O  R  Y    Ce

          6 5 3 2 1
          . . .                        .
      ([6]1)2 1 6 5 3         (5[r]6)1   6 5 3 2
                                            .
                               5     1   6 5   2

                             3 2 1r              6 5
                                                 . .

                             3(2 1)2   1         6 5
                                                 . .

                             3     2   1(r)6 5 6 5
                                         . . . .
```

Figure 11 (continued)

Manyura   Sanga

```
          C   A   T   E   G   O   R   Y    Cf

(3 1)    3    2 1

         3(r)2 1

3 1 3 2 3   2 1

         3    2 1 2 1(r)

2 1 6 1 2 3   2 1            1r6 1 2 1 6r
    .                            .
         3 5 3 2r           (3 2)3    2 1

                            3r    2 1

         5 3r2r             3    2 1r

                            3 2 1 2 1

                            5 3 2r

         6(r)5 3            5r3 2

6r5 6   5 3
 .   .
   1 6 1 6 5r

(6)2   1 6                     5 1 6 5
 .       .                       .
                                 .
   1 2   1 6(r)             6 1 6 5(r)
          .                    .

                           6 1r6 5
                             .
2 1 2(r)1 6                6 1 6 1 6 5
         .                  . .   . .

                           5 6 1 6 5
                               .
```

41

Figure 11 (continued)

Manyura	Sanga

```
C   A   T   E   G   O   R   Y      Cg

        (6)2  1
           ·

              2  1r
    ([3]2)3  2

                              6  5
                              ·  ·
                              3  2r
```

```
C   A   T   E   G   O   R   Y      Ch

  3 2     1 2r        2  1  6  1(r)
                            ·
  3 2(r)1  2

      2     1 2(r)

  2 3     1 2
```

```
C   A   T   E   G   O   R   Y      Ci

        2  3  2
```

Key:

    r = repeated
    (x) = x is optional
    (x[y]) = xy and y are optional

Figure 12. Occurrence of Ambiguous Final Patterns in Sléndro Pathet Manyura and Sléndro Pathet Sanga Gendhing

Final Patterns (cipher notation)	Category	Occurrence in Manyura	Occurrence in Sanga
˙˙ 612	Be	2	3
12	Bf	2	2
6532	Cc	1	4
3216 ˙	Cc	1	1
321	Cf	2	4
32121	Cf	1	2

Total number of final patterns in pathet manyura 109
Total number of final patterns in pathet sanga 158

Figure 13. Two Similar Final Patterns in Sléndro Pathet Manyura and Sléndro Pathet Sanga

Cèngkok 1, from Ladrang *Pangkur*, Sléndro Pathet Manyura:

```
 ..   .   . ...        —    —
.12 3  .3 121 6/    .3 2 . 121
       M 2.2           M or S Cf
```

Cèngkok 2, from Gendhing *Gambir Sawit*, Sléndro Pathet Sanga:

```
             —  —
1 2/ .  .3 212 1
S Sh    M or S Cf
```

Unlike the initial patterns in Figure 9, a particular final contour in Figure 11 often is realized on several different pitch levels. For example, contour Ba is realized as

```
              3
           2
        1
     6
     .
```

and as

```
                    .
                 1
              6
           5
        3
```

in pathet manyura.

For the most part, like initial patterns, final patterns are differentiated by pathet. For example, a typical final pattern of a pathet manyura 6 cèngkok is

```
     3    3
           2
        1    1
              6
              .
```

whereas a typical final pattern of a pathet sanga 6 cèngkok is

```
           3
        2    2
              1
              6
              .
```

Mode in Javanese Music

A few final patterns, however, are found in both pathet manyura and in pathet sanga, such as

$$6 \ 5 \ 3 \ 2 \ (Cc), \ 6 \ \overset{\cdot}{1} \ \overset{\cdot}{2} \ (Be) \ \text{and} \ 3 \ 2 \ 1 \ (Cf)$$

Most of the ambiguous final patterns occur very infrequently in the data, as illustrated in Figure 12 (p. 43).

Furthermore, these ambiguous final patterns are almost always combined with initial patterns whose pathet is not ambiguous. For example, although the two cèngkok in Figure 13 (p. 44) have the same final patterns, the pathet of each cèngkok is clear from the initial pattern. The patterns in Figure 13 are labelled in the following way: The first symbol, that is *M*, *S*, or *M or S*, indicates that the pattern is found exclusively in pathet manyura gendhing, or exclusively in pathet sanga gendhing, or in gendhing of both pathet. Following the pathet designation, a series of numbers refers to an initial pattern in Figure 9, while a series of letters refers to a final pattern in Figure 11.

Short Cèngkok

Short cèngkok, the second kind of cèngkok, consist of either (1) a short initial pattern, usually one to three notes, and a final pattern or (2) merely a final pattern. When a poetic line is only four syllables or less, the pesindhèn usually chooses a short sindhèn cèngkok. It is significant that the initial part of a sindhèn cèngkok, not the final part, is abbreviated when a shorter cèngkok is needed. Shortening the initial part is consistent with the Javanese conception of beginnings as weak stress or dhing and endings as strong stress or dhong, (see p. 17–18). For the same reason, while the initial pattern is sometimes entirely omitted, a final pattern is always present.

46

Figure 14. Short Initial Patterns in Sléndro Pathet Manyura and Sléndro Pathet Sanga

Manyura Patterns (cipher notation)	Number of Occurrences	Sanga Patterns (cipher notation)	Number of Occurrences
		$\overset{\bullet}{2}6$	1
		$\overset{\bullet}{5}1$	1
3	1	2	2
		2r	1
$2\overset{\bullet\bullet}{3}$ or $\overset{\bullet\bullet}{2}3$	23	1$\overset{\bullet\bullet}{2}$ or $\overset{\bullet\bullet}{1}2$	26
$\overset{\bullet}{1}$r$\overset{\bullet\bullet}{2}3$	2		
		2r32r	1
		53	2
6	1		
56	4	35	3
		235	1

47

Short initial patterns found in all the pathet manyura and sanga gendhing in Appendices 2–3 are listed in Figure 14 (p. 47).[5] Figure 15 illustrates a short initial pattern followed by a final pattern.

Figure 15.　An Excerpt from Ketawang *Puspa Warna*, Sléndro Pathet Manyura

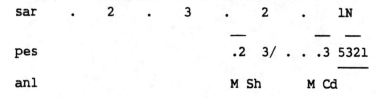

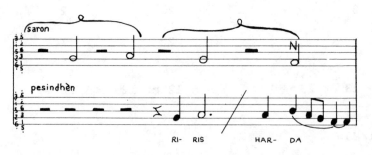

Within the short cèngkok, initial patterns are governed by the first principle of pathet. The most common pathet sanga short initial pattern

$$2$$
$$1$$

is lowered one pitch level from the most common pathet manyura short initial pattern

$$3$$
$$2$$

Furthermore, none of the fifteen short initial patterns are used both in pathet manyura and in pathet sanga.[6]

Plèsèdan Cèngkok

Plèsèdan cèngkok, the third kind of cèngkok, are sung when certain kinds of melodies are sung by the gérong or dhalang, or played on the saron, rebab or *bonang* (a set of pot gongs). These melodies alter the usual manner of singing.

Ordinarily, the last pitch level of a sindhèn cèngkok matches the last pitch level of the saron gatra in which the cèngkok is being sung. The final tone of a gatra or of a cèngkok is called a *sèlèh* tone, labelled S. If pitch levels other than the sèlèh tone of the gatra are emphasized in the next gatra, a *plèsèdan cèngkok* is usually sung. This cèngkok ends on the pitch level emphasized in that next gatra, as Figure 16 (p. 50) illustrates. Although the sèlèh tone of the gatra is pitch level 6, the pesindhèn may not sing a cèngkok that ends on pitch level 6. She must sing a cèngkok that ends on pitch level 2, which is repeated by the saron in the following gatra. Although the repetition of a pitch level in the following gatra usually occurs in the saron part, immediate repetition of a pitch level in the bonang, rebab, gérong, or dhalang parts may also dictate the use of a plèsèdan cèngkok.[7]

Figure 16. A Plèsèdan Cèngkok from Gendhing *Gambir Sawit*, Sléndro Pathet Sanga

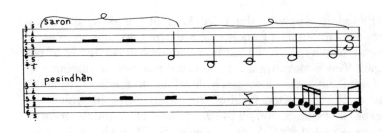

For singing plèsèdan, the pesindhèn has three choices: (1) she can sing one cèngkok consisting of three patterns, (2) she can sing two cèngkok, or (3) she can sing one cèngkok consisting of two patterns, an initial pattern and a final pattern.[8]

Plèsèdan: Type I. The pesindhèn sings an initial pattern, a middle pattern (which is either a final pattern or a repeated note) and a final pattern (which ends on the same pitch level as the repeated pitch level in the following gatra).

Figure 17 (p. 52) illustrates the first method of singing plèsèdan, in which the middle pattern is also a final pattern. The initial pattern

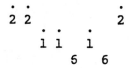

is followed by a final pattern ending on pitch level 5, and the cèngkok ends with another final pattern

$$
\begin{matrix}
& \overset{\bullet}{2} \\
\overset{\bullet}{1} & \\
6 &
\end{matrix}
$$

The last pitch level of the cèngkok (pitch level 2) conforms to the pitch level repeated in the gatra *after* the sèlèh tone, rather than the sèlèh tone (pitch level 6).

The second method of singing type 1 plèsèdan is illustrated in Figure 18 (p. 53). An initial pattern (sanga 2.1) is followed by a middle pattern that consists of a series of repeated tones (pitch level 5). The third pattern is a final pattern from Figure 11 (sanga Cd), and the cèngkok ends on the pitch level repeated in the gatra after the sèlèh tone (pitch level 2).

51

Figure 17. Plèsèdan Singing: One Cèngkok of Three
Patterns from Gendhing *Gambir Sawit*,
Sléndro Pathet Sanga

```
sar    .    .    3̇    2̇    .    1̇    2̇    6 S

pes                  2  2.1  161  .6  2/2.6  1.65/

anl                       S 3.1       S P Ca


sar    2̈    2̈    .    .

pes    6.12̈

anl    M or S Be
```

52

Figure 18. Plèsèdan Singing: One Cèngkok of an Initial Pattern, Repeated Note and Final Pattern from Gendhing *Gambir Sawit*, Sléndro Pathet Sanga

```
          .
sar       1              6              5              3N S
          . .   .                .      _              _
pes       1 2 . 1      6 1. / 5 5/    .535          6.5
anl             S 2.1        S P     S Cd


sar       2              2              .              .

pes      3.2
         ___
```

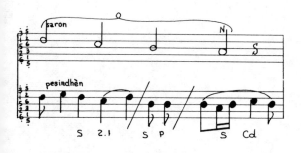

Figure 19.   Plèsèdan Singing: Two Cèngkok from
Ketawang *Suksma Ilang*, Sléndro Pathet
Manyura (Sindhèn Cèngkok by Ki
Wasitodipuro)

```
                     .   .   .   .
sar    3   5   6    1P   3   2   1    6G S
                      ‾‾ ‾‾ ‾‾  ‾‾
                     .  . .  . . ..
pes                 .2 3.5 3.212./653.66//
                    ‾‾‾‾‾ ‾‾  ‾‾‾
txt                 Lala- na jajah negari

anl                     M 2.3      M Aa


       .   .
sar    1   1   .   .

            .
pes    63.561
       ‾‾‾‾‾
txt    Rama

anl    M Ba
```

Figure 19 (continued)

/ separates patterns within a cèngkok
// separates one cèngkok from another

Plèsèdan: Type II. The pesindhèn sings two cèngkok. The first cèngkok consists of an initial pattern and of a final pattern that ends on the same pitch level as the sèlèh tone. The second cèngkok consists of only a final pattern ending on the pitch level repeated in the gatra after the sèlèh tone. Figure 19 illustrates this type of plèsèdan singing. Comparing Figure 19 with Figure 17 (p. 52), one might wonder why I labelled the three patterns of Figure 17 as one cèngkok, whereas I divided the three patterns of Figure 19 into two cèngkok. I did this for two reasons: (1) The second pattern (M Aa) in Figure 19 ends on the pitch level of the sèlèh tone, signalling the completion of a standard cèngkok of one initial and one final pattern. The second pattern (S P Ca)

55

in Figure 17 does not end on the pitch level of the sèlèh tone. (2) Two poetic lines are used in Figure 19, one for each cèngkok. Only one poetic line is used in Figure 17.

Plèsèdan: Type III. The third manner of singing plèsèdan is somewhat rare in my data, and occurs only in the books by Gitosaprodjo. The pesindhèn sings a cèngkok of two patterns (an initial pattern and a final pattern, which comprise one poetic line), but the last pitch level of the cèngkok matches the pitch level that is repeated in the gatra after the sèlèh tone, as illustrated by Figure 20 (p. 57).

The first principle of sindhèn pathet (pathet sanga cèngkok are lowered one pitch level from pathet manyura cèngkok) governs plèsèdan cèngkok. The initial and final patterns used in plèsèdan cèngkok are the same as initial and final patterns used in non-plèsèdan cèngkok. Middle patterns, if they occur, also conform to the first principle of pathet. For type I (in which all three patterns are sung as one cèngkok), when the middle pattern is a final pattern, it usually ends on pitch level 6 (or sometimes on pitch level 3) in pathet manyura. In pathet sanga, the middle pattern usually ends on pitch level 5 (or sometimes on pitch level 2), pitch levels lowered one step from those used in pathet manyura. When the middle pattern consists of a repeated tone (as in Figure 18, p. 53), pitch level 6 in pathet manyura and pitch level 5 in pathet sanga are always used.

Figure 20. Plèsèdan Singing: One Cèngkok of Two Patterns from Ladrang *Sri Wibawa*, Sléndro Pathet Sanga

```
sar     2     2     .     .     5     3     2     1N S

                                    · ·
pes                             565161 52/232 16
                                ‾‾‾‾‾‾        ‾  ·
anl                              S 1.3     S Cd


sar     6     6     .     .

pes     1 6
        ‾‾‾
         ·
```

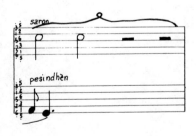

Figure 21. A Non-Plèsèdan Cèngkok of Three Patterns from Gendhing *Gambir Sawit*, Sléndro Pathet Sanga

```
                     .
sar    .    .    .   1    .    .    .    6 S

                     .. .. . ‾.
pes                  12.32.16.1/.55.3.2/2.3.5.6

anl                  S 2.3       S Cf    S Be


sar    .    .    .   3

pes    6
```

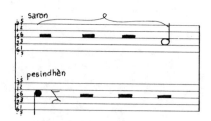

Figure 22. Similar Contours in Pairs of Sléndro Pathet Manyura and Sléndro Pathet Sanga Cèngkok

Source	Gendhing	Pathet	Cèngkok

Gitosaprodjo — Gendhing *Kawit* — Manyura

```
3 3           3/ 3
    2 2              2
        1        1  1
                        6
                        .
```

Gitosaprodjo — Ketawang *Sinom Parijata* — Sanga

```
2 2           2/ 2
    1 1              1
        6        6  6
        .        .  .
                        5
                        .
```

Wasitodipuro — Ladrang *Pangkur* — Manyura

```
              .
              3
        .  .  .
        2  2  2
              .
              1
                 6
                    5
                    3/   3
                         2
                            1
```

Gitosaprodjo — Ladrang *Sri Wibawa* — Sanga

```
           .
           2
        .  .  .
        1  1  1
              6
                 5
                    3
                2/ 2   2
                         1
                            6
                            .
```

Figure 22 (continued)

Source	Gendhing	Pathet	Cèngkok

Tukinem — Ketawang *Suksma Ilang* — Manyura

```
              3
          .   .   .
          2   2   2/
                  .            .
                  1            1
                      6 6 6      6
                          5    5
                            3/ 3
```

Wasitodipuro — Gendhing *Gambir Sawit* — Sanga

```
              .
              2
          .   .   .
          1   1   1/
                  6            6
                      5 5    5
                          3  3
                            2/ 2
```

Tukinem — Ketawang *Suksma Ilang* — Manyura

```
                          3
              2 ·       2
          1   1   1
                  6/
                  .
```

Wasitodipuro — Gendhing *Gambir Sawit* — Sanga

```
                          2
              1         1
          6   6   6
          .   .   5/  .
                  .
```

Figure 22 (continued)

Source	Gendhing	Pathet	Cengkok

Tukinem   *Srepegan*   Manyura

$$\dot{2}/$$
$$\dot{1}$$
$$6 \; 6 \qquad 6$$
$$5$$
$$3$$

Tukinem   *Srepegan*   Sanga

$$\dot{1}/$$
$$6$$
$$5 \; 5 \qquad 5$$
$$3$$
$$2$$

Wasitodipuro   Ketawang *Puspa Warna*   Manyura

$$\dot{3}$$
$$\dot{2} \qquad \dot{2}/$$
$$\dot{1}$$
$$6 \qquad 6 \; 6$$
$$5$$
$$3$$

Wasitodipuro   Gendhing *Gambir Sawit*   Sanga

$$\dot{2}$$
$$\dot{1} \; \dot{1} \; \dot{1}/$$
$$6$$
$$5 \qquad 5 \; 5$$
$$3$$
$$2$$

Non-Plèsèdan Cèngkok of Three Patterns

The fourth kind of cèngkok, non-plèsèdan of cèngkok of three patterns, occur occasionally in the data. In such cèngkok, the last pitch level matches the sèlèh tone rather than any pitch level in the following gatra. For example, the cèngkok in Figure 21 (p. 58) has three patterns, but ends on pitch level 6, the sèlèh tone. Cèngkok of this type are also governed by the first principle of sindhèn pathet: All of them end on pitch level

$$\overset{\textstyle .}{1}$$

in pathet manyura and on pitch level

6

in pathet sanga.

PRINCIPLE I AND THE RELATIONSHIP OF PATTERNS WITHIN THE CÈNGKOK

I have shown how principle I operates paradigmatically by explaining how patterns in the same category (e.g., short initial pathet manyura patterns) relate to one another. Now I will demonstrate how principle I operates syntagmatically by describing the way in which patterns of different categories are strung together to form a cèngkok.

For example, the pathet manyura initial patterns in category 1 of Figure 9 (pp. 29–31) are combined only with pathet manyura final patterns whose last pitch levels are

$$3, \ 2, \ \overset{\textstyle .}{1}, \ \text{or } 1$$

Likewise, the pathet sanga initial patterns in category 1 are combined only with pathet sanga final patterns whose last pitch levels are one pitch level lower, i.e., pitch levels

$$2, \ 1, \ 6, \ \text{or} \ \overset{\bullet}{6}$$

The pathet manyura category 2 initial patterns in Figure 9 are used with final patterns of pitch levels

$$\overset{\bullet}{6}, \ \overset{\bullet}{1}, \ 1, \ 2, \ \overset{\bullet}{2}, \ \text{or} \ 3$$

and for pathet sanga with final patterns of pitch levels

$$5, \ 6, \ \underset{\bullet}{\overset{\bullet}{6}}, \ 1, \ \overset{\bullet}{1}, \ \text{or} \ 2$$

The pathet manyura initial patterns in category 3 are combined primarily with final patterns of pitch levels

$$6 \ \text{or} \ \overset{\bullet}{6}$$

and for pathet sanga with final patterns of pitch level[9]

$$5 \ \text{or} \ \underset{\bullet}{5}$$

Gitosaprodjo (no date a:2) articulates the theory that pathet sanga cèngkok are formed by lowering pathet manyura cèngkok one pitch level. Figure 22 (pp. 59–61) shows that sindhèn cèngkok from both Tukinem's and Ki Wasitodipuro's music also reflect this relationship between pathet manyura and pathet sanga.

Mode in Javanese Music

PRINCIPLE II

The first principle of pathet deals only with pathet manyura and pathet sanga gendhing. The second principle concerns pathet nem: sindhèn cèngkok found in pathet nem gendhing consist of pathet manyura cèngkok, of pathet sanga cèngkok, and occasionally of cèngkok that belong exclusively to pathet nem.

This principle can be tested by examining the sindhèn cèngkok in the pathet nem gendhing in Appendix 4. I have labelled all the sindhèn patterns either pathet manyura, pathet sanga, or pathet nem, with letters and numbers referring to long initial, short initial, and final patterns found in Figures 9, 14, and 11 respectively. For example, the cèngkok

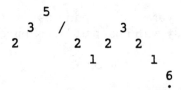

in Ladrang *Remeng*, pathet nem, is analyzed as *S Sh / S Cd*. The first pattern is a pathet sanga short initial pattern listed in Figure 14 (p. 47). The final pattern is very similar to

$$
\begin{array}{cccc}
 & 3 & & \\
2 & & 2 & \\
 & & 1 & \\
 & & & 6 \\
 & & & \bullet
\end{array}
$$

found in category Cd in pathet sanga of Figure 11.

Almost all of the cèngkok in these pathet nem gendhing are either pathet manyura or pathet sanga cèngkok, as the second principle of pathet states. There are more pathet manyura patterns, however, than pathet sanga patterns in pathet nem gendhing (206 pathet manyura patterns, as opposed to 31 pathet sanga patterns). In fact, some gendhing in pathet nem, such as Gendhing *Majemuk*, include only pathet manyura sindhèn cèngkok. This ambiguity between pathet manyura and pathet nem in my data reflects the difficulty that Javanese musicians sometimes have in distinguishing pathet nem gendhing and pathet manyura gendhing.

Although most of the cèngkok in the pathet nem gendhing appear in my corpus of pathet manyura and pathet sanga gendhing, there are some patterns in the pathet nem gendhing that do not appear in that corpus. There are six occurrences of a pattern that does not appear in my corpus of pathet manyura or pathet sanga gendhing. I have classified this pattern as pathet nem. All the other patterns occurring in pathet nem gendhing are probably rare pathet manyura or pathet sanga patterns. They are marked with question marks in Appendix 4 since evidence for determining the pathet of these patterns is insufficient. To distinguish between a pathet nem pattern and a rare pathet manyura or pathet sanga pattern, I have used the following method.

An initial pattern in a pathet nem gendhing that possesses the following two properties is probably a pathet nem pattern, a pattern unacceptable in a pathet manyura or a pathet sanga gendhing: (1) The initial pattern does not appear in my corpus of initial patterns of pathet manyura and pathet sanga gendhing. (2) The initial pattern is combined both with a final pattern found in pathet manyura gendhing but not in pathet sanga gendhing, and (in another cèngkok) with a final pattern found in pathet sanga gendhing but not in pathet manyura gendhing. The second property is not possessed by any of the pathet manyura initial patterns in my corpus of pathet manyura gendhing or by any of the pathet sanga initial patterns in my corpus of pathet sanga gendhing. Furthermore, in my corpus of pathet nem gendhing, that property is not possessed by any of the initial patterns identified as manyura or sanga.[10] Therefore, if an initial pattern appearing in a pathet nem gendhing but not in my corpus of pathet manyura or pathet sanga gendhing has this property, there is good reason not to classify it as manyura or sanga, but rather as nem.

In my corpus of pathet nem gendhing, there are six occurrences of an initial pattern that meet the requirements 1 and 2 above for a pathet nem pattern. This pattern occurs in four different gendhing (appearing twice in two of those gendhing), and these gendhing are notated or sung by three different sources. This unusual pattern is, therefore, not merely the peculiarity of one gendhing or the creation of one pesindhèn. It appears twice in Ladrang *Krawitan* (sindhèn cèngkok by Gitosaprodjo) and twice in Gendhing *Kabor* (sindhèn cèngkok by Tukinem):

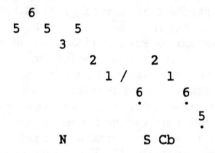

Here it is combined with a final pattern that is found exclusively in pathet sanga gendhing. In Ladrang *Remeng* (sindhèn cèngkok by Ki Wasitodipuro), a very similar initial pattern is again combined with a final pattern that is found exclusively in pathet sanga:

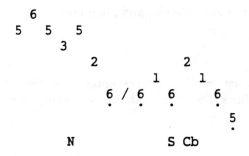

In a slightly different form, the same initial pattern appears in Gendhing *Lokananta* (sindhèn cèngkok by Ki Wasitodipuro) combined with a final pattern that is found exclusively in pathet manyura:

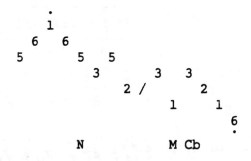

The pitch level

$$\overset{\bullet}{1}$$

in this pattern distinguishes this pattern from the other pathet nem initial patterns listed above. I believe, however, that this pattern is essentially the same as the other initial patterns, because that pitch level is an unimportant trill tone. The notes

$$\overset{\bullet}{6}16$$

67

are all sung to one syllable, and pitch level

$$\dot{1}$$

is sung very quickly, represented notationally by two horizontal lines placed over that pitch level, as illustrated in Figure 23.

Figure 23.   A Sléndro Pathet Nem Initial Pattern from Gendhing *Lokananta*

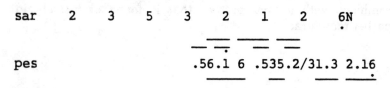

```
sar     2     3     5     3     2     1     2    6N
                                                  .
                      __    __    __    __
                    ___   _.__   __    __
pes                .56.1 6 .535.2/31.3 2.16
                                     __    __
                                              .
```

The other initial and final patterns of pathet nem gendhing that do not appear in my corpus of pathet manyura and pathet sanga gendhing are marked with question marks in Appendix 4. A few of these are final patterns without initial patterns. Since they are not combined with patterns from either pathet manyura or pathet sanga, there is not enough evidence to know if such patterns are pathet nem patterns or rare pathet manyura or pathet sanga patterns. The rest of the patterns marked with question marks in

68

Appendix 4 are combined with initial or final patterns used exclusively in either pathet manyura or pathet sanga gendhing. These patterns, however, are never combined both with patterns used exclusively in pathet manyura and with patterns used exclusively in pathet sanga. Thus these patterns are probably rare pathet manyura or pathet sanga patterns, although I have labelled them only with question marks in Appendix 4.

With this discussion of the pathet system of sindhèn patterns as background, it is possible to devise a method for determining the pathet of a gendhing based on the sindhèn cèngkok. In the next chapter, the sindhèn method of pathet determination will be first described and then compared to other methods of pathet determination.

CHAPTER 4

PATHET PREDICTION

PATHET PREDICTION IN SINDHÈN CÈNGKOK

The simplicity of the sindhèn system of pathet as illustrated by the two pathet principles discussed earlier makes pathet determination both easy and accurate. I have selected for pathet analysis three gendhing sung by two pesindhèn not yet represented in this study: Ketawang *Sekar Téja* sung by Ngabéhi Mardusari of Surakarta, Gendhing *Kocak* and Ladrang *Dirada Meta*, both sung by Soepadmi Soetomo of Surakarta. (See Appendix 5 for transcriptions of these gendhing.) By using Figures 9, 11, and 14, where long initial, final, and short initial patterns are listed respectively, I am able to determine the pathet of these three gendhing. Examining the sindhèn cèngkok of gendhing sung by pesindhèn not represented in this study yields a few patterns not present in Figures 9, 11, and 14, but nevertheless the pathet of the gendhing are easy to determine.

In Ketawang *Sekar Téja*, all the cèngkok of the first three gongan are in pathet manyura. Although there are some ambiguous final patterns, all are combined with initial patterns whose pathet is clearly manyura. The initial pattern of the plèsèdan cèngkok at the last gong tone

71

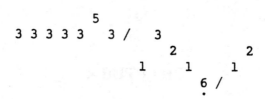

essentially consists of a series of 3's. In Figure 14, the short initial pattern, pitch level 3, occurs only in pathet manyura; thus I have labelled that pattern as "M Sh."

In summary, Ketawang *Sekar Téja* cannot be in pathet sanga. Since all the cèngkok are in pathet manyura, it is not likely that the gendhing is in pathet nem: most gendhing in pathet nem would include some pathet sanga sindhèn cèngkok, as illustrated in Appendix 4. The conclusion that Ketawang *Sekar Téja* is in pathet manyura is, in fact, correct (Gitosaprodjo 1972b:42).

In Gendhing *Kocak* both pathet manyura and pathet sanga cèngkok are used, indicating that the gendhing is in pathet nem. The presence of the one cèngkok that my data indicates is used exclusively in pathet nem (seen at the second kenong) supports this argument (see p. 226). Two types of relatively rare cèngkok appear in Gendhing *Kocak*: *gawan* and *barang miring*. I have not analyzed these types of cèngkok in terms of pathet since they are governed by completely different rules of pitch, rhythm, and contour from other sindhèn cèngkok (see Appendix 1, pp. 93–95). Most of the patterns used in Gendhing *Kocak* appear in Figures 9 and 11 (pp. 29–31 and 37–42).

As in Gendhing *Kocak*, the sindhèn cèngkok in Ladrang *Dirada Meta* indicate pathet nem. Pathet nem is not as clearly defined in Ladrang *Dirada Meta*, however, since all of the cèngkok are in pathet manyura until the last gongan when two pathet sanga cèngkok appear. The final pattern of the cèngkok near the second gong (see p. 230)

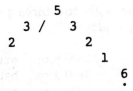

does not occur in Figure 11 as a manyura pattern. It probably is a pathet manyura pattern, however, because the pathet sanga counterpart to this pattern does appear in category Ce:

$$
\begin{array}{c}
3 \\
\quad 2 \\
\quad\quad 1 \\
\quad\quad\quad 6 \\
\quad\quad\quad \cdot\; 5 \\
\quad\quad\quad\quad \cdot
\end{array}
$$

Perhaps had I had a larger sample of pathet manyura gendhing, this infrequent pattern would have appeared.

Since Javanese musicians characterize the pathet of Gendhing *Kocak* and Ladrang *Dirada Meta* as pathet nem (Sumarsam, personal communication, and Probohardjono 1957:13–14), I can conclude again that hearing the sindhèn cèngkok of a gendhing is often sufficient evidence to determine the pathet of the gendhing.

Now that the pathet system of sindhènan is clear, it is possible to compare that system with (1) Javanese definitions of pathet and (2) the pathet system of saron gatra.

JAVANESE DEFINITIONS OF PATHET

The theory of pathet based on an analysis of sléndro sindhèn cèngkok presented in this study is consistent with a common Javanese definition of pathet. The three sléndro pathet are associated with the three periods of a *wayang kulit*, or shadow puppet play:

9:00 p.m.	−	12:00 p.m.,	pathet nem
12:00 p.m.	−	3:00 a.m.,	pathet sanga
3:00 a.m.	−	6:00 a.m.,	pathet manyura

Most of the pieces played in a given period of the night are in the pathet designated for that period. As the play progresses, the vocal range of the *dhalang*, or puppeteer, becomes increasingly high. Thus many Javanese theorists define pathet in terms of range, as the "place of a gendhing" (Purbodiningrat 1956:200)[1] or as the "highness and lowness of pitches" (Gitosaprodjo 1971a:6).[2] In the following table, the middle column illustrates the ranges that are characteristic of the three sléndro pathet (Gitosaprodjo 1971a:6). (The instruments that use these ranges are not specified.) In the right column, the ranges of the sindhèn cèngkok found in my data are listed for each pathet.

Pathet	Gitosaprodjo	Sindhèn Cèngkok
nem	235612356123	5612356123
sanga	561235612	561235612(3)
manyura	35612356123	35612356123(5)

The sindhèn ranges coincide almost exactly with Gitosaprodjo's ranges, and the minor discrepancies are easily explained. Since it is difficult for most pesindhèn to sing lower than a pitch level

5

very few sindhèn cèngkok include pitch levels

$$\overset{\bullet}{2} \text{ or } \overset{\bullet}{3}$$

In fact, Gitosaprodjo (1971b:3) even says that pitch levels

$$\overset{\bullet}{2} \text{ and } \overset{\bullet}{3}$$

cannot be sung by the pesindhèn. However, both in Gendhing *Kocak* and in Ladrang *Dirada Meta* (in pathet nem), Soepadmi Soetomo does sing those two pitch levels. Thus if these two gendhing had been included in the data rather than being used as test cases, the pathet nem range for sindhèn cèngkok would have been exactly like Gitosaprodjo's range. For the most part, the highest tones in pathet sanga and pathet manyura are pitch levels

$$\overset{\bullet}{2} \text{ and } \overset{\bullet}{3}$$

respectively. Occasionally the upper neighbor trill tones, pitch levels

$$\overset{\bullet}{3} \text{ and } \overset{\bullet}{5}$$

are used for pathet sanga and pathet manyura, respectively, as illustrated in Figure 24. Pitch level

$$\overset{\bullet}{5}$$

in the cèngkok is sung briefly, as the notation indicates.

Figure 24.   A Cèngkok from Gendhing *Perkutut Manggung*, Sléndro Pathet Manyura

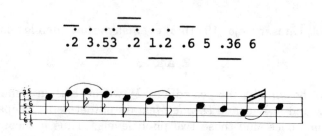

.2 3.53 .2 1.2 .6 5 .36 6

PATHET PREDICTION IN SARON GATRA— THE INFORMATION MEASURE

In analyzing the pathet system for saron gatra, Becker (1980) speaks of the determinants of pathet, the features of saron gatra important in determining the pathet of the gendhing in which the gatra are found. Becker suggests three determinants of pathet for saron gatra:

1. the melodic contour or shape of the saron gatra;
2. the pitch level on which that contour is realized, that is, the last pitch of the gatra, called the *end-pitch level*;
3. the position of the gatra in the formal structure of the composition, in relation to *gong position*, *kenong position*, or other position, called *kempul position*.

In reference to the third determinant of pathet, the gong marks the most important point in the formal structure, that is, the end point. Gong position is the gatra whose last beat is marked by a stroke on the gong. A series of gatra marked at the end by a gong is called a *gongan*. The kenong, of secondary importance, divides the gongan into two or four parts, depending on the gendhing structure, and a series of gatra marked at the end by a kenong is a *kenongan*. Although the kenong always plays whenever the gong plays, kenong position refers only to those points at which the kenong plays alone. The kempul further subdivides the kenongan.[3] In Becker and Templeton's analysis, kempul position refers not only to those gatra at which the kempul is struck, but also to all other gatra not marked by kenong and gong. Thus kempul position is a catch-all category for the levels of lesser importance of the formal structure.

In analyzing Becker's data, Templeton (1980) calculated the amount of information that melodic contour and pitch level of saron gatra in the three positions of the formal structure provide with respect to pathet. This information is expressed in a number ranging from 0 to 1, with numbers close to 0 representing relatively little information, and numbers close to 1 representing high information. For example, the gatra 3232 in gong position occurs once in pathet manyura, never in pathet sanga, and fifteen times in pathet nem. Thus we would expect a relatively high information value for this gatra when it occurs in gong position, for we know that the gendhing cannot be in pathet sanga. Indeed the information value is quite high, .8221. On the other hand, if a gatra occurs about equally in a given position in each of the three pathet, the information value is low. Such is the case for the gatra 3532 in kempul position, which occurs twenty-three times in pathet manyura, thirty-four times in pathet sanga, and sixteen times in pathet nem. The information value is .0403.

By calculating the accumulative information of the saron gatra used in twenty-two sléndro gendhing, Templeton was able to determine correctly the pathet of eighteen of those gendhing. The four errors were all confusions between pathet nem and pathet manyura. Since distinguishing pathet nem and pathet manyura is difficult for the Javanese themselves, the informational analysis proves to be a fairly accurate tool for determining the pathet of gendhing.

PATHET PREDICTION IN SINDHÈN CÈNGKOK— THE INFORMATION MEASURE

An informational analysis of sindhèn cèngkok is not necessary to determine the pathet of a gendhing. Unlike saron gatra, sindhèn patterns are almost exclusively associated with either pathet manyura or pathet sanga. Thus, the only source of ambiguity lies between pathet manyura and pathet nem, as noted above.

Although sindhèn cèngkok are effective indicators of the pathet of a gendhing, an informational analysis of sindhèn pattern contour and pitch in the three positions of the formal structure will enable us to compare the pathet system of sindhèn patterns to the pathet system of saron gatra. This analysis will reveal to us (1) the relative importance of pitch and contour in determining the pathet of sindhèn patterns, (2) the pathet information provided by contour alone and pitch alone of sindhèn patterns, and (3) whether position in the formal structure is a determinant of pathet for sindhèn patterns.

The results of the informational analysis of sindhèn patterns and saron gatra in the three sléndro pathet are presented in Figure 25. The average information in sindhèn patterns and saron gatra of both pitch level alone and contour alone are shown for each structural position.[4]

Figure 25 reveals that both contour and pitch level alone provide substantial amount of pathet information for saron gatra. Contour provides more information than does end-pitch level for saron gatra, for the information values of saron gatra contour are consistently higher than those for saron gatra end-pitch level.

It would seem that the best way to determine the relative importance of contour and pitch in sindhèn patterns would be to perform the same kind of analysis on sindhèn patterns that was performed on saron gatra.[5] Such an analysis is easily done for sindhèn contour. An analysis of only the last pitch level of each sindhèn cèngkok, however, would not provide

Figure 25. Average Information with Respect to Sléndro Pathet Contained in Sindhèn Patterns and Saron Gatra in Each of the Three Positions in the Gong Cycle

Position	Saron Gatra		Sindhèn Patterns	
	End-Pitch Level	Contour	Pitch Level per Sindhèn Pattern	Contour
Gong	.3638	.4272	.1945	.0722
Kenong	.1393	.2825	.0432	.0372
Kempul	.0273	.2364	.0671	.0994

information about sindhèn cèngkok *per se*, for the last pitch level of a sindhèn cèngkok is, with the exception of the plèsèdan cèngkok, dictated by the last note of the saron gatra. Instead, I have found the average amount of pitch information per sindhèn pattern for a sample of thirty-six sindhèn patterns. These patterns represent the two most common initial patterns and the two most common final patterns in each of three positions in the gong cycle in each of three pathet. This analysis required two steps. I analyzed the degree to which each pitch level at a particular position is associated with pathet over the entire corpus of gendhing. Secondly, using an algorithmic procedure (Templeton 1980:214–6), I analyzed the degree to which each pitch level in a particular sindhèn pattern is associated with pathet, conditioned on all the pitch levels that preceded it in the pattern. For example, the pattern

3 3   3
    2 2
       1

was chosen for analysis as the most common initial pattern at gong position in pathet manyura. Before analyzing this pattern *per se*, I calculated the probabilities with which each of the pitch levels at gong position are associated with the three pathet. Using this information, I then calculated the total amount of pitch information in that pattern at gong position. The information value for this pattern at gong position (.4939) was then averaged with the information values for the eleven other patterns chosen for analysis at gong position, to obtain an average information level per sindhèn pattern at gong position.

The resulting information values for sindhèn pitch level reveal that there is some information provided by pitch, but only at gong position, which will be explained presently. That there is any information provided by pitch at all can be explained by the fact that pitch level 3 in pathet sanga and pitch level 5 in pathet manyura are restricted. Some Western scholars of Javanese music have referred to these tones in these pathet as *enemy tones* (Hood 1954:245). It is no coincidence that the pathet sanga restricted tone is one pitch level lower than the pathet manyura restricted tone. This analysis supports earlier findings that the lowering of pathet manyura produces pathet sanga. On the average, pitch level 3 represents 8.4% of sindhèn pitch levels in pathet sanga in my corpus, and pitch level 5 represents 7.9% of all pitch levels in pathet manyura, whereas if the six pitch levels were evenly distributed in each pathet, one would expect figures of about 17%. In fact, by calculating the percentage occurrence of pitch levels 3 and 5 for a gendhing of unknown pathet, one can frequently determine the pathet of the gendhing.[6]

The resulting information values for sindhèn contour are so low that we can conclude that there is no association of contour with pathet for sindhèn patterns.

Figure 25 reveals that position plays only a small role in sindhèn pathet determination. The differences between the average information values at all three positions for contour and the difference between the average information values at kenong and kempul positions for pitch level are insignificant. This indicates that knowing the position of contours at all three positions or the position of pitch levels at kenong and kempul positions does not add significantly to the listener's knowledge of the pathet of the gendhing. There is some information provided by pitch level at gong position, however, which can be explained by the reduplication of certain pitch levels at gong and by the prevalence of certain pitch levels as gong tones in the saron melody.[7]

Position plays a much less important role in pathet determination for sindhèn patterns than position plays for saron gatra. The greatest difference between the average information values for pitch level at a given position is only .1514 for sindhèn patterns (the average information value at gong minus the average information value for kenong). In contrast, for saron gatra, the greatest difference between the average information values for end-pitch level at a given position is significantly higher: .3365.

PATHET SYSTEMS COMPARED

In conclusion, the similarities between the two systems of pathet, saron and sindhèn, are far outweighed by the differences. Among the similarities is the fact that, in both systems, pathet sanga is the most easily distinguished pathet. In addition, only a few saron gatra show a high correlation (i.e., an information of .5 or more) with pathet nem, while more gatra have a high correlation with pathet manyura and pathet sanga. Similarly, there is only one sindhèn pattern that is associated exclusively with pathet nem, while there are many patterns that are associated exclusively with either pathet manyura or pathet sanga.

The most basic difference between the two systems of pathet is that pathet manyura sindhèn cèngkok can be lowered one pitch level to produce pathet sanga cèngkok, and that, for the most part, the cèngkok used in pathet nem gendhing are a combination of pathet manyura and pathet sanga cèngkok. As Templeton illustrates, these two factors do not operate for saron gatra, except for rare cases like Ladrang *Pangkur* where the pathet sanga version is one step lower that the pathet manyura one.

The relative importance of the three determinants of pathet (pitch level, contour, and position) also differ in the two systems of pathet. In sindhèn cèngkok, pitch level is a more important determinant of pathet than is contour, at least for making some basic distinctions. For the saron system, Templeton states that "...with regard to sub-elements of *gatra*, melodic contour plays a more important role than pitch level in determining *pathet*" (1980:198). The third determinant of pathet—position—is important for saron, but not for sindhèn.

CHAPTER FIVE

DIFFERENT SYSTEMS OF PATHET

IN THE GAMELAN

It would appear that in gamelan music there are at least two different systems of pathet operating. With respect to saron gatra, there are three separate sléndro pathet whose determinants are pitch, contour, and position. With respect to sindhèn cèngkok, there is basically one pathet, pathet manyura, which by transference to lower pitch levels yields another pathet: pathet sanga. When those two pathet are combined, a third pathet emerges: pathet nem. Furthermore, the only determinant of pathet for sindhèn cèngkok, which alone is important, is pitch, for pitch levels 3 and 5 often indicate the pathet.

How do the pathet systems of the other gamelan instruments compare to the pathet systems for sindhèn cèngkok and for saron gatra? R. L. Martopangrawit suggests the following:

For Ladrang *Pangkur* in sléndro pathet manyura and Ladrang *Pangkur* in sléndro pathet sanga, the vocal melodies might possibly be the same, but the instrumental melodies certainly would be different.

This statement can be proved if we study the bonang. The pathet manyura bonang part for Ladrang *Pangkur* is inappropriate for Ladrang *Pangkur* in sléndro pathet sanga. This means that the part cannot merely be shifted up or down, which is known as transposition in Western music (1972:vol.1a,50).[1]

In the first paragraph, Martopangrawit means that the contours of the vocal cèngkok would be the same in the pathet manyura and pathet sanga versions of Ladrang *Pangkur*, for the pathet manyura cèngkok would be "transposed" (to use his term in the second paragraph) down one step to produce pathet sanga cèngkok. The pathet manyura and pathet sanga versions of the bonang part for Ladrang *Pangkur*, however, are not related to one another in this way.

Although Martopangrawit says in the first paragraph of the passage quoted above that pathet manyura "instrumental melodies" cannot be shifted down to produce pathet sanga melodies, it is clear from another passage that he is not referring to all instrumental melodies, for in the following passage he is discussing the pathet system of the gendèr.

> The question has occasionally been asked as to whether new cèngkok could be created by merely raising and lowering the pitch levels of existing cèngkok, that is, transposition. My answer to this is that it would be difficult. It is possible to transpose a pathet manyura cèngkok down one pitch level to produce a pathet sanga cèngkok, for example. Only occasionally, there will be a cèngkok that is forced (1972:vol.1b,12).[2]

From this statement, it appears that the pathet system for gendèr is like that for sindhèn, but different from the saron and bonang pathet system. Gitosaprodjo suggests that pathet manyura cèngkok are lowered one pitch level to produce pathet sanga cèngkok for the rebab (1970b:87),[3] gendèr (1970a:7), *suling*, an end-blown bamboo flute (1971c:1), and *celempung*, a zither (1971a:20), while Sutton's data support the same relationship between pathet manyura and pathet sanga for gambang (1975:117–25, 128–48, 224–6, 240, 254–57).

Thus I conclude that there are two somewhat different systems of pathet in the gamelan. In one system (for sindhèn, rebab, gendèr, suling, celempung, and gambang) pathet sanga cèngkok are created by lowering pathet manyura cèngkok, while for the other system (for bonang and saron) pathet sanga cèngkok cannot be created in that way.

From a Western standpoint, the existence of two systems of mode within one ensemble is surprising. However, the simultaneous operation of diverse concepts within one context is a hallmark of Javanese music and even of Javanese culture as a whole.[4]

SPECULATIONS ON THE HISTORY OF PATHET

How did two somewhat different systems of pathet arise? Kunst's theory of the existence of two ensembles during the latter part of the Hindu-Javanese period could account for these two systems. One ensemble consisted of "loud-sounding instruments" such as bonang, kendhang, and gongs, and was used for outdoor performances, in processions, at ceremonials, and in war. The other ensemble consisted of "soft-sounding instruments" such as gendèr, rebab, suling, and gambang, and was intended for indoor use (and probably for wayang kulit too). According to Kunst (1973:113–8), these two ensembles were probably combined at the earliest at the end of the Hindu-Javanese period during the last part of the fifteenth century.

Evidence for the validity of Kunst's theory is that ensembles of exclusively loud and exclusively soft-sounding instruments still exist today as separate entities, in addition to the combined ensembles. The soft-sounding instruments are used almost exclusively in both *gamelan gadhon* and *sulukan*. The former includes all the instruments of the complete ensemble except bonang, saron, and gong ageng. For sulukan, short poems sung by the dhalang in a wayang performance, only rebab, gendèr, gambang, and suling are used. Ensembles of exclusively loud-sounding instruments also still exist today: *Gendhing bonang* employ only bonang, saron, slenthem[5] and various gongs and drums. The musical accompaniment for certain court dances (such as *beksa lawung* and *beksa Madura*) and for hobby horse dances (such as *reyog* and *jaran képang*) also consists of exclusively loud-sounding instruments.

Although I feel confident in the basic validity of Kunst's theory, some counter-evidence exists. Warsadiningrat, in his book on the history of gamelan (*Wédha Pradangga*, 1979:vol1, pp. 3,6 and in press) and Pakubuwana X (in *Noot Gending lan Tembang* c.1926:6 and in press) both suggest that centuries before the fifteenth century a single ensemble included both loud and soft-sounding instruments. It is difficult, however, to interpret these statements within a Western historical framework. There are old Balinese ensembles (*caruk* and *gambang*) that include both loud and soft-sounding instruments, as well as singing, in the case of the gambang ensemble. Yet, we do not know how old these ensembles are.

Although on further research Kunst's theory may prove to be oversimplified, let us assume for the present that the theory on the whole is correct, for doing so suggests some interesting ideas on the possible development of the sindhèn system of pathet. The reader should be warned that the section that follows is meant only to point the way to new avenues of research, not to state definitively how the sindhèn system of pathet developed.

If Kunst's theory is correct, we can assume that before the merging of the loud and soft-sounding ensembles, vocal music was used exclusively with the soft-sounding instruments for the following reason. Today vocal music plays an important (if not dominant) role in those ensembles of exclusively soft-sounding instruments, while it is totally absent in the exclusively loud-sounding ensembles. The saron is associated with the loud-sounding instruments, and from the historical evidence of the *gamelan sekati*, it has played this role for several hundred years.

All the soft-sounding instruments (gendèr, rebab, suling, celempung, gambang and the voice) are precisely the instruments that today use one system of pathet, while the loud-sounding instruments (bonang and saron) use the other system of pathet. Before the merging of the two ensembles, possibly two systems of pathet were in use, and those two systems have been maintained (although in modified form) in the modern-day ensemble.

What might the determinants of pathet for loud and soft-sounding instruments have been prior to the merging of the two ensembles? It is clear that neither system of pathet presently in use is the same as earlier systems, as the unusual use of pathet in the *gendhing sekati*, played on the gamelan sekati, reveals (Toth 1970:76–78). Prior to the fifteenth century, the concept of pathet may not yet have been articulated, but we can still ask what rules of pitch or contour organization were in operation for those old ensembles. The music played on the most archaic ensembles that we know of, *gamelan monggang* and *gamelan kodhok ngorèk*, which are loud style ensembles, is not classified according to pathet. Perhaps the beginnings of the concept of pathet can be seen in the way that pitch is correlated with subdivision in the gong cycle. Those ensembles do not have any saron; rather the principal instrument is the bonang. Since the bonang in the modern-day gamelan very frequently plays the same tones as the saron, though in a different rhythm, statements about the pitch organization of the bonang part for the archaic ensembles may be relevant to the pitch organization of the saron and bonang melodies of modern ensembles. Hoffman shows how a particular pitch is associated exclusively with a particular level of subdivision in the gong cycles for Gendhing *Monggang* and Gendhing *Kodhok Ngorèk*. Exact correspondence between pitch and level of subdivision is also evident in some of the melodies of more modern gendhing, such as the first gongan of Ketawang *Suba Kastawa* (Figure 26, p. 88), as Hoffman points out (1975:49). Pitch level 1 occurs only at the level of kethuk, while pitch levels 6 and 5 occur only at kempul and kenong levels respectively.

In the system of pathet used for saron gatra, position in the gong cycle is an important determinant of pathet.

Figure 26. Pitch and Level of Subdivision in Ketawang *Suba Kastawa*

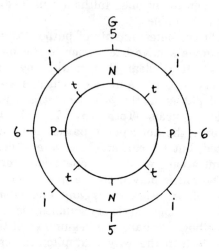

g = gong   p = kempul   n = kenong   t = kethuk

Perhaps this is so because modern saron and bonang melodies have retained some of the characteristics of the archaic melodies in which there was a one-to-one correspondence between pitch and level of subdivision in the gong cycle. Although position in the gong structure (gong position, kenong position, and kempul position) is not exactly the same as level of subdivision, they are clearly very closely related. In both Gendhing *Monggang* and in modern saron melodies, rules about what pitches or contours can be played are partly, or wholly in the case of Gendhing *Monggang*, determined by the position of those pitches or contours in the gong cycle.

I suggest that position is not a determinant of pathet for sindhèn melodies because vocal melodies were originally not part of cycles whose subdivisions are marked by gongs. Hoffman (1975:16) emphasizes that vocal melodies differ markedly from the melodies of archaic gong ensembles: ". . . they [vocal melodies] are linearly conceived melodic lines, the contours and pitches of which neither are dependent upon nor in any way mark the subdivisions of a temporal cycle." By vocal melodies, Hoffman means sung poetic forms such as *macapat, kidung* and *sulukan.* Since such melodies were originally not part of a gong structure, position in a gong structure could not possibly be a determinant of pathet.

Although I am not claiming that sindhèn melodies derived from any of the sung poetic traditions mentioned above, they are vocal melodies, and as such, may be governed by similar rules. The precursors of the modern-day pesindhèn, the *talèdhèk*, who were street singers and dancers, did not organize their singing around gong, kenong and kempul tones. On the contrary, "they sang wherever they liked" (Ki Wasitodipuro, personal communication). Furthermore, the repertoire of gendhing associated with the talèdhèk (called *gendhing talèdhèkan* or *gendhing parikan*) is characterized by unusual gong structures—kenongan of unequal lengths, gongan of only three kenongan, etc. (Kunst 1973:282, 303–4).[6] In such gong structures, gong, kenong, and kempul do not mark binary subdivisions in a gongan. As further evidence that historically talèdhèk singing was not governed by gong cycles, Ki Wasitodipuro mentioned to me that pesindhèn from the villages (where talèdhèk singing originated) do not understand where the gong, kenong, and kempul appear in the formal structure. This also suggests that the village pesindhèn, not having exposure to court gamelan traditions where gong subdivision music is paramount, reverts to her original training in sindhènan which does not include instruction in gong, kenong, and kempul placement. According to Ijzerdraat (1959:14), the pesindhèn, or talèdhèk was not permitted to sing in the full gamelan until the middle of the last century. Thus the music of the talèdhèk was not associated with cycles in which subdivisions are marked by gongs.[7] It is not surprising, then, that in the pathet system for sindhènan, position in the gong cycle is not a determinant of pathet.

The possible historical existence of two different gamelan ensembles, loud and soft, may explain (1) the development of two systems of pathet in the modern-day ensemble, as well as (2) the importance of position as a determinant of pathet for saron gatra and its absence in the sindhèn system of pathet.

The importance of pathet manyura in the sindhèn system of pathet may be related to the fact that pathet manyura seems also to be the basic pathet for rebab and gendèr, the two instruments in the gamelan most closely associated with sindhènan. The beginning rebab and gendèr student always is taught pathet manyura gendhing first. Also, as I noted earlier, pathet sanga cèngkok for rebab and gendèr are said by the Javanese to be created by lowering pathet manyura cèngkok one pitch level. So closely associated is sindhènan to rebab and gendèr that beginning pesindhèn students are told to listen to those instruments to decide what cèngkok to sing. It is even possible to sing an unknown gendhing merely by listening to the cèngkok of the rebab or gendèr. Thus, according to this theory, since vocal music has long been associated with gendèr and rebab, it was natural for the pesindhèn to model her pathet system after that of the gendèr and rebab when she started singing in the full gamelan.

However, this leaves us with the question: why might the pathet system for gendèr and rebab be based on pathet manyura? This question might be answered when we reflect that the gendèr and rebab are the most important instruments in wayang music. The gendèr is played almost continuously throughout the entire performance. It has the important function of constantly informing the dhalang of the principal tones of the pathet in use at the time. Rebab and gendèr provide the primary instrumental accompaniment to the dhalang's singing, in pieces known as *pathetan*.

The strong association that gendèr and rebab have with wayang is relevant to the pathet system of those instruments, since pathet manyura can be considered to be the most important pathet of a wayang. The *talu*, musical introduction to the wayang, is in pathet manyura. Even though the first section of a wayang is nominally in pathet nem, the first gendhing is often *Ayak-ayakan* in pathet manyura, and many pathet manyura gendhing are played during the pathet nem section. Furthermore, since pathet nem and pathet manyura are often ambiguous, the distinction between pathet nem gendhing and pathet manyura gendhing in this section of the wayang becomes even more hazy. The third, and thus the last, section of the wayang is also in pathet manyura, and so the wayang begins and ends in pathet manyura. During Kunst's research in Java (*ca.* 1920's-40's) even the middle section of a wayang, which is nominally in pathet sanga, included some pathet manyura gendhing, for gendhing talèd-hèkan in pathet manyura were played during that section to accompany the dancing and singing of the *punakawan*, or clown-servants (Kunst 1973:303-4). This is no longer true today, when virtually all gendhing in that section are either in sléndro pathet sanga or pélog pathet nem. Thus the importance of pathet manyura in the wayang could account for its importance in the pathet systems for gendèr and rebab.

Kunst's theory also suggests an explanation for the fact that pathet manyura is not primary in the pathet system for saron gatra. The saron, as a loud-sounding instrument, was probably not associated with vocal music until recently (with the merging of the two ensembles), and thus it did not share the vocal system of pathet. The saron may not have been played in the wayang until the merging of the two ensembles either.[8] Perhaps the concept of pathet originally developed as a vocal phenomenon in the context of the dhalang's singing pathetan. Even the word "pathetan," deriving as it does from the root *pathet*, suggests that pathet is fundamentally associated with vocal music in the wayang. Perhaps an old system in which pitch marked subdivisions in gong cycles merged with the vocal system of pathet, resulting in the system of pathet used by the saron today. In fact, the complexity of the saron system—which involves three different pathet—as opposed to the simplicity of the sindhèn system which involves basically only one pathet transposed—is understandable in light of the combination of two systems of organizing pitch and contour. No overall definition of pathet can be given, as two different systems of pathet are in operation in gamelan music.

APPENDIX 1

UNUSUAL CÈNGKOK

There are three unusual kinds of cèngkok that occasionally appear in the data: *barang miring*, *gawan* and what I call *rujak*. I have not identified initial and final patterns in these cèngkok nor included them in my analysis of pathet since they are governed by different rules of pitch, contour and rhythm from standard cèngkok. These cèngkok are merely labelled according to their cèngkok type in Appendices 2–5.

Barang miring cèngkok (sung only in gendhing in laras sléndro) include pitches other than the five sléndro pitches. Of the approximately thirty barang miring cèngkok that appear in my data, most have the following contour:

```
                    -
                -
        - -         -
                -           -   -
                    -   -   -       -
                    - /              -
```

This contour is realized on pitch levels 6 and 2, producing the cèngkok

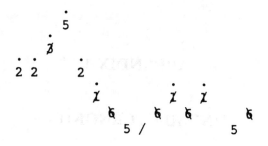

and

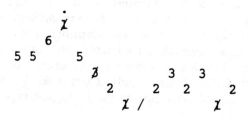

The numbers with a slash down to the left indicate a pitch somewhat higher than the same number without a slash, while the numbers with a slash down to the right indicate a lower pitch. The initial pattern of the first cèngkok remotely resembles the pathet manyura initial pattern 2.3 (Figure 9)

$$\begin{array}{ccc} & 5 & \\ 3 & & 3 \\ 2 & & 2 \end{array}$$

This barang miring cèngkok, however, never appears in pathet manyura, only in pathet sanga and in pathet nem. The contour of the final pattern is nothing like most of the final patterns in Figure 11, which either descend or ascend.

A gawan cèngkok is (1) a cèngkok peculiar to a specific gendhing or (2) a cèngkok associated exclusively with a particular set of words (Gitosaprodjo 1971b:5). In my data,

Appendix 1: Unusual Cèngkok

only the first type of gawan cèngkok appears. Gawan
cèngkok usually follow the saron melody quite closely both
rhythmically and melodically, as illustrated in Figure 27.

Figure 27.   Two Gawan Cèngkok from Gendhing
Majemuk, Sléndro Pathet Nem

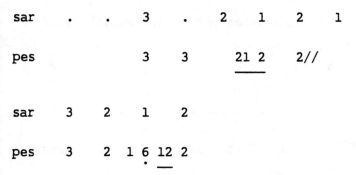

sar	.	.	3	.	2	1	2	1
pes			3	3	21 2	2//		

sar	3	2	1	2	
pes	3	2	1 6	12 2	

Figure 28.   Two Rujak Cèngkok from Ladrang *Asmara Dana*, Sléndro Pathet Manyura

```
sar     2              3              2              1

pes         2   2   3   3   3   3   3   2   2   3   2   1

txt         Rujak nanas pantes dèn wadahi gelas


sar     3              2              1              6
                                                     .

pes         1   2   2   2   2   2   3   3   1   2   1   6
                                                        .

txt         Tiwas tiwas nglabuhi wong ora welas
```

RUJAK NA NAS PANTES DÈN WADAHI GELAS

TI WAS TI·WAS NGLABUHI WONG ORA WELAS

96

Appendix 1

Rujak cèngkok differ from standard sindhèn cèngkok both textually and musically. Instead of singing wangsalan (see pp. 16–18), the pesindhèn sings a related poetic form of two lines of twelve syllables each, called *parikan*. In most of the parikan sung today by pesindhèn, different kinds of *rujak* (fruit salad) are mentioned with humorous intent. Assonance plays an important role in parikan. Musically, rujak cèngkok differ from standard sindhèn cèngkok in three ways: (1) Rujak cèngkok are sung in syllabic style as opposed to the melismatic style of most sindhèn cèngkok. (2) Whereas the rhythmic relationship of standard cèngkok to the saron melody is loose, rujak cèngkok follow the rhythm of the saron melody closely. (3) Rujak cèngkok employ many more repeated tones than do standard cèngkok. Figure 28 illustrates a pair of rujak cèngkok.

INTRODUCTORY REMARKS

TO APPENDICES 2, 3, 4, AND 5

All the gendhing used for the purpose of this study are notated in Appendices 2, 3, 4, and 5. The sources for the gendhing are listed in the references by the musician responsible for the sindhèn cèngkok. All gendhing associated with Gitosaprodjo are in his "Sindenan Titilaras Tjakepan" (no date b). Within each appendix, the gendhing are listed alphabetically by title. Introductions to gendhing, called *buka*, are not included in the notation. Gitosaprodjo and Ki Wasitodipuro sometimes use dots indicating range in the saron melody; the other sources do not use dots. Using *Gending-Gending* by R. Ng. S. Probohardjono as the authority, I have added the missing dots.

Below the saron melody, the sindhèn cèngkok and text are notated. Two cèngkok or two texts are notated below some saron gatra because upon repetition of a gendhing, the pesindhèn often sings different cèngkok or texts. All the cèngkok, but not all the texts, used in the original sources have been included. One diagonal line (/) divides the cèngkok into patterns. Two diagonal lines (//) separate one cèngkok from another, when the division is not otherwise clear. Since the texts are in a somewhat archaic language and since the primary means of passing the texts from one pesindhèn to another is oral, there are various versions of some of the texts. Rather than choosing one version and claiming it as standard, I have for the most part retained each pesindhèn's version of the texts. Commas in the text indicate separation between the text used for one cèngkok and the text used for the next cèngkok, when the division is not otherwise clear. Capital letters in the text usually indicate the beginning of a new poetic line or new line of isèn-isèn text. Capital letters sometimes occur in the middle of what appears to be one poetic line because the text for a single cèngkok can consist of two poetic lines. All capital letters do not signify the beginning of new poetic lines, however, for proper names occasionally appear in the texts. Symbols below the cèngkok identify (1) the pathet of the pattern and (2) long initial, final, and short initial patterns listed in Figures 9, 11, and 14. These symbols are labelled "analysis," abbreviated "anl."

M = pathet manyura
S = pathet sanga
N = pathet nem
Numbers below sindhèn cèngkok = long initial pattern (Figure 9).
Letters below sindhèn cèngkok = final pattern (Figure 11).
Sh = short initial pattern (Figure 14).
P = plèsèdan
? = pattern does not appear in Figures 9, 11 and 14.
Barang miring = see Appendix 1
Gawan = see Appendix 1
Rujak = see Appendix 1

Other symbols and terms used in the notation are listed below:
G = gong
GS = gong suwukan, smaller than the gong.
N = kenong
P = kempul
Umpak = first section of some gendhing, preceding the ngelik section.
Ngelik = a high-registered section of some gendhing.
Suwuk = final section of a gendhing.
Minggah = second section of some types of gendhing.
[: :] = this section is repeated.

GENDHING IN SLÉNDRO MANYURA

WITH SINDHÈN NOTATION

Ladrang *Asmara Dana*, Sléndro Pathet Manyura
(Sindhèn Cèngkok by Gitosaprodjo)

sar	2	1	2	6	2	1	2	3N

sar	5	3	2	1P	$\overset{\bullet}{3}$	$\overset{\bullet}{2}$	$\overset{\bullet}{3}$	$\overset{\bullet}{1}$N
pes					6	$\overset{\bullet}{1}$ $\overset{\bullet}{2}$.	6/	$\overset{\bullet}{3561}$
txt					Sen-	dhon	nèn-dra	
anl						M 1.1	M Ba	

sar	6	3	2	1P	3	2	1	6N
pes						232	1 2 / 6 5 .3 6 6	
txt						Arané re -	si wa-na-ra	
anl						M 2.1	M Aa	

sar	5	3	2	1P	3	2	1	6G
pes					3333 3 3 22 1 3/.3 1 21 6			
txt					Haywa mundur Wong Anom labuh nagara			
anl					M 3.1	M Ca		

sar	2	1	2	6	2	1	2	3N
pes						6 1 2/ . 6165 5 3		
txt						Jeruk gan- da		
anl						M 1.1 M Cd		

sar	5	3	2	1P	3	2	3	1N
pes					232 12 .6 3/.3561 1			
txt					Busana geming Pandi- ta			
anl					M 2.1 M Ba			

102

Appendix 2: Pathet Manyura

```
sar    6      3      2      1P     3      2      1      6N
                                   . .        . .    . .
pes                                2 3  / . 3 1    21 6
                                               ‾‾   ‾‾‾
txt                                Anu  -   ru - ta

anl                                M Sh     M Ca


                                                      N
sar    5      3      2      1P     3      2      1     6G
                                                       .
pes                                3322 1 3/.13 2.16
                                          ‾‾   ‾‾‾‾ ·
txt                                Obahing jaman samantya*

anl                                M 3.1     M Cb
```

Minggah

```
sar    2      3      2      1      3      2      1      6
                                                        .
pes    2 2 3 33 3 3 2 2/ 321       1 2 2 22 2 3/3 1 2 16
                                                          .
txt    Rujak nanas pantes          Tiwas tiwas nglabuhi
       dèn wadahi gelas,            wong ora welas
anl              Rujak                        Rujak


sar    2      3      2      1      1      3      6      3N
                                   .      . . .        .
pes                                616  212.6 /6. 6165 3
                                         ‾‾       ‾‾‾
txt                                Anjasmara a- ri ma-  mi

anl                                M 1.3     M Cd
```

---

*This word appears as "samangkya" in other versions of this wangsalan.

103

```
sar    6     1·    3·    2·    6      3      2     1P
                               ···   ··
pes                            232   12 . 63/ .353 21
                                    ‾‾            ‾‾
txt                            Mas mirah kulaka  war-ta
anl                                   M 2.1      M Cd


sar    3     5     3     2     5      3      2     1N
                               ···   ··             ·   ·
pes                            232   12. 63/. 3561  1
                                    ‾‾           ‾‾
txt                            Dasihé tan wurung la-  yon
anl                                   M 2.1      M Ba


sar    6     1·    3·    2·    6      3      2     1P
                                ·    ···
pes                            616  212. 6 3/.353 21
                                    ‾‾          ‾‾ ‾‾
txt                            Anèng kutha Praba lingga
anl                                   M 1.3      M Cd


sar    3     5     3     2     5      6      1·    6N
pes                            3 2 2 1 3/.13   216
                                      ‾‾      ‾‾·
txt                            Tandhing lan Uru bis-ma
anl                                   M 3.1      M Cb
```

Appendix 2: *Pathet Manyura*

```
                                    .
sar    5      3      5      3      1      6      2      1P

                                  ... ..
pes                               232 12.  6 3/   353 21
                                      ‾               ‾
txt                               Karia muk- ti wong a-yu

anl                                    M 2.1      M Cd



                                                        N
sar    .      3      .      2      .      1      .      6G
                                                        .

pes                               3 3 2 2 13/. 31  2.16
                                             ‾     ‾
                                                     .
txt                               Pun kakang pamit palastra

anl                                    M 3.1      M Ca
```

Ayak-ayakan, Sléndro Pathet Manyura
(Sindhèn Cèngkok from R. Soetrisno's Wayang Kulit *Bima Suci*)

```
                                                        N
sar                                                    2G


                                  N                     N
sar    .      3N     .      2GS    .      3N     .      2GS


                                  N                     N
sar    .      5N     .      3GS    .      2N     .      1GS

pes                                          2   3/   2 1 1//
                                                      ‾
txt                                          Ta-was   pi- ta

anl                                          M Sh   M Cg
```

105

```
                         N                              N
sar    2      3N    2    1GS   2     3N    2    1GS


                         N                              N
sar    3      5N    3    2GS   3     5N    3    2GS
       .    . . .
pes   6 1 6 2 1 2 6 3/ 3 6 5 3 2
          ‾‾‾    ‾ ‾‾‾
txt   Darpa driya Wisnu gar-wa

anl        M 1.3        M Cb


                         N                              N
sar    5      3N    5    6GS   5     3N    5    6GS
       .      .    .     .     .     .     .     .
pes       2  321/    3 2 1  6 6
             ‾‾      ‾‾‾‾‾‾‾ . .
txt   Mur - wèng    gi  -  ta

anl        M 2.1        M or S Cc


                         N                              N
sar    5      3N    5    6GS   5     3N    2    3GS
       .      .    .     .
pes       2  3/   121  6/  1   2      3
                  ‾‾‾‾‾‾‾‾‾ .
txt       Ya ra - ma

anl       M Sh   M P Cf      M Be
```

Appendix 2: Pathet Manyura

```
                               N                         N
sar    6       5N      3      2GS     3       5N      3      2GS

                  ..
pesl      6  12  6/  5  53   6  32  2//        2   1   6/    1    2
                 ——           ——                       ·
txtl   Kar-sa da-lem Sri Naréndra,          Go    -    nès

anll      M 1.1       M Cb                   M Cf       M or S Bf
                                        .   .   .
pes2                                     1   2   2  6   3/ 3212  2
                                                      ——
txt2                                    -Éman   é  -  man  é -  man

anl2                                         M 1.1        M Ch


                               N                         N
sar    3       5N      3      2GS     5       3N      2      3GS

pes                       2  3/  21    2  16/  123
                             ——            ·    ——
txt                       Riris har - da

anl                       M Sh      M P Cf    M Be


                               N                         N
sar    2       1N      2      1GS     2       3N      2      1GS

pesl     3  3  2  2  1  3/  32121   1//    2  5  3  2  6 /  2  1
                        ——                 ——             ·
txtl   Hardaning wong lumaksana           Go-nès wi-ca - ra-né

anll       M 3.1        M Cf                 M 2.3        M Cg

pesl                                      2  3 /  6  5  3    2  1
                                             ——              ——
txt2                                      Gonas ga  -   nès

anl2                                      S Sh        M Ce
```

107

```
                              N                           N
sar   2      3N      2      1GS    3      5N      3      2GS

                                         .  .  .
pes                                   6  1  2  1  6  / 3 212
                                         ‾‾‾‾‾‾‾
txt                                   Dresing        karsa

anl                                      M 1.1       M Ch


                              N                           N
sar   3      5N      3      2GS    5      3N      5      6GS
                                  .      .       .       .
pes          2   1   6/  1    2//    3 3 2 2 3 1/ 2 1 6  6
                     .                          ‾‾‾‾ .   .
txt          Ra-ma                   Mamayu hayuning Pra- ja

anl          M Cf  M or S Bf             M 3.1       M Cf


                              N                           N
sar   5      3N      5      6GS    5      3N      5      6GS
      .      .       .       .     .      .       .       .
pes                                   2   3 / 1   2    1   6/
                                                ‾‾‾‾‾‾‾‾‾‾ .
txt                                   Ya ra- ma

anl                                   M Sh       M P Cf


                              N                           N
sar   5      3N      2      3GS    6      5N      3      2GS
                                         .  .
pes1   1  2  3//                      6  1  2 6/ 53536 5 3 2//
       ‾‾‾‾‾                           ‾‾‾‾‾      ‾‾‾‾‾
txt1                                  Rama      ra - ma

anl1     M Be                         M 1.1       M Cb
                                      .  .
pes2                                  1  1 6 5 3/  6   5
                                            ‾‾‾    ‾‾‾
txt2                                  Rama rama    ra-

anl2                                     M 4.1   M or S P Cc
```

Suwuk:

```
                            N                        N
sar    1      1N      2    1GS    3     2N    1     6GS
                                                     .
pes      3  2 /  3   2   1//*  3  3  2  2  3  1 /2 1 6 6
                                                   .  .
txt            ma          Ma-ma-yu-ha-yuning Pra- ja

anl         M or S Cf            M 3.1           M Cf
```

Ayak-ayakan with Ngelik, Sléndro Pathet Manyura
(Sindhèn Cèngkok by Tukinem)

```
                                                     N
                                                    2GS


                        N                        N
sar    .     3N    .    2GS    .     3N    .     2GS


                        N                        N
sar    .     5N    .    3GS    .     2N          1GS

pes                            2      3/    2 1  1

txt                            Ri  -  ris   har- da

anl                             M Sh       M Cg
```

---

*This cèngkok occurs only before the suwuk. This particular suwuk is played only after 6532GS.

```
                               N                              N
sar    2      3N     2       1GS    2      3N     2         1GS
                                                          .
pes                 2  3/  21 1//                     6  1  6
                            ——
txt               Rama    rama                        Hardaning

anl             M Sh   M Cg


                               N                              N
sar    3      5N     3       2GS    3      5N     3         2GS
       .
pes    2  6 3/  3   2  1   2//                2     3/  212 2//
                   ———                                   ———
txt  wong lumak-sa - na                        Ra - ma  ra-ma

anl  M 1.3        M Ch                          M Sh     M Ch


       .            .                .                        .
sar    5      3N     5       6GS    5      3N     5         6GS
       .            .                .            .          .
pes             2  3/ 1 321 6  6              2  3/ 31 2 1 6
                      ———— . .                      —       .
txt          Dresing kar -  sa               Radèn ra-dèn

anl           M Sh    M Cb                    M Sh     M Ca


       .            .                N                        .N
sar    5      3N     5       6GS+   3      5N     6         1GS
       .            .                .
pes                               6   6  5  3  5  6       1//
                                     ——————————————————
txt                               Yo   mas

anl                                              M Ba
```

Appendix 2: Pathet Manyura

```
                          .N      .            .      .N
sar    3      5N     6    1GS     2     6N     1      2GS

                                  .             .      .
pes               6   65356  1//  6     6       1      2//
                      _____
txt              Yo mas            Go- nès

anl                 M Ba                  M or S Be



       .                  N                         N
sar    1      6N     5    6GS     5      3N     5    6GS

       . . .  ..
pes    2 3 2  12/  6 5 3 6  6//        3  / 5 3 2  3 5  6
               __    __                     _____
txt    Mamayu hayuning Pra-ja          Ra - ma

anl    M 2.1      M Aa                 M Sh       M Ba



                          N                          .N
sar    5      3N     5    6GS     3      5N     6     1GS

                                                      .
pes                               6   6 5  3 5    6    1//
                                      _____
txt                               Yo   mas

anl                                        M Ba



                          .N      .            .      .N
sar    3      5N     6    1GS     2     6N     1      2GS

                          .                    .      .
pes           6   6 5 3 5 61//    6             6   1  2//
              _____               _____
txt          Go-nès,              Ra  -  ma

anl              M Ba                    M or S Be
```

111

```
                                    N                                N
sar     1       6N      5         6GS       5       3N      5      6GS

          .       .       .   .   .
pes       2      3/      1   2   1 6 //           3/  5 3 2 3 5 6
                                                        _____
txt       Ku  -  su    mas-tra                    Ra- ma

anl          M Sh      M Ca              M Sh      M Ba



                                    N                                N
sar     5       3N      5         6GS+      5       3N      2      3GS

                                      .   .   .       .   .
pes                               2   3   3 2 1 6     1   2
                                          _____     ___
txt                               Care-ming           rèh

anl                                          M 2.1



                                    N                                N
sar     6       5N      3         2GS       3       5N      3      2GS

pes       6    3/  3 6   6 53532//                2 3 / 212 2
                   ___   ____                           ___
txt       pa-la- kra- ma                          Radèn ra- dèn

anl                    M Cb                        M Sh    M Ch



                                    N                                N
sar     3       5N      3         2GS       5       3N      2      3GS

                                                          .
pes                     2 3/  31 216/ 1 2 3//          6  1
                              __  .          ___         _
txt                     Moring gendhing               Pi-na-

anl                     M Sh  M P Ca     M Be
```

112

Appendix 2: Pathet Manyura

```
sar     2       1N      2       1GS*

pes        2̇    6   3 2   16123/21  1
                          ·̣
txt           tut lawan wi -  ra-ma

anl              M 1.1        M Cg
```

Gendhing *Kawit*, Kethuk 2 Kerep, Minggah Ladrang, Sléndro Pathet Manyura
(Sindhèn Cèngkok by Gitosaprodjo)

```
sar     .       .       .       3       .       1       2       3

pes                                             1       2       3

txt                                             Ya      ra  -   ma

anl                                                   Gawan


sar     .       1       2       3       .       1       2       3N

pes             1       2       3//          3 3̷     3 2     3

txt             Ya      gen  -  dhuk        Jarwa    mu  -   dha

anl                   Gawan                      Barang Miring
```

---

*The ngelik is played in *Ayak-ayakan* pathet manyura only during the
talu, the introduction to the wayang kulit. In this transcription, the ngelik
appears between the two signs +.

113

```
sar     2       2       .       .       2       2       3       2

pes     2                                       2  3/ 1  2       2
        -
txt                                             Jarwa mu   -    dha
anl                                             M Sh       M Bf


                                                                    N
sar     3       5       6       5       3       2       1          2G

pes                                             3 3 3 3 . 3 2 23  2

txt                                     Mudhané Sang Prabu Kresna

anl                                             Barang Miring


sar     .       .       2       .       2       2       3       2

pes1                                            2 3/  1  2       2

txt1                                            Pupung a   -    nom

anl1                                            M Sh       M Bf

pes2                                            2 3/  2 1  2      2

txt2                                            Pupung a   -    nom

anl2                                            M Sh      M Ch


sar     3       5       6       5       3       2       1       2N
                                                   ...
pes                                           6   1216 /3     212

txt                                           Pu - pung a  -   nom

anl                                                M 1.1      M Ch
```

Appendix 2: Pathet Manyura

```
sar    3      3      .      .      3      3      5      3

pes1   3//                              5   6/   6  1  6  5 3
                                                    .
txt1                                    Pupung a    -    nom
an11                                    M Sh        M Cd
                                             ..     .
pes2                                    6  12/  6   1  6  5 3
txt2                                    Pupung a    -    nom
an12                                    M 1.1       M Cd


                                                           N
sar    .      6      .      1      2      3      5       3G

pes                                6 6 6ø  6 3   3 ž 23  3
txt                                Ngudi sarananing Pra- ja
an1                                       Barang Miring


Minggah

                                  .
sar    5      3      5      6     i      6      5      3N
                                        . .    .
pes                                6    1 2 /  6165    3
txt                                Sendhon    nèn -    dra
an1                                M 1.1      M Cd
```

115

```
                            .
sar   5     3     5    6P   1     6      5      3N
                             .   ...         .
pes                         6 1 6 212 6. 6/ 6165 3/
                                   ___        __ _
txt                         Arané re- si wa-na - ra
anl                                 M 1.3      M P Cd


sar   2     2     .    .P   2     2      3      2N
pes    2  3  2//                 2 3/  1  2     2
                                      ___
txt                          Haywa  mun  -  dur
anl       M Ci                   M Sh    M Bf


                                                 N
sar   3     5     6    5P   3     2      1      2G
                            .   ...
pes                         6 1 6 212 6 3/.212  2
                                   ___      ___
txt                         Wong anom labuh wanara
anl                                 M 1.3    M Ch


sar   3     2     3    5    6     5      3      2N
                                 ...
pes                              6 1216  /3    212
                                   ____        ___
txt                              Je-ruk  gan- da
anl                                    M 1.1   M Ch
```

Appendix 2: Pathet Manyura

```
sar    3      2      3      5P     6      5      3      2N
                                    .      ...
pes                                6 1 6 212 6 3/.212  2
                                        ___      __    _
txt                                Busana geming pandhita
anl                                     M 1.3      M P Ch


sar    3      3      .      .P     3      3      5      3N
                                                 .
pes   1 6/1 2 3                          5  6 /  6 1 6 5 3
       ___.___                                  _____
txt                                      A- nu    ru  -  ta
anl        M Be                          M Sh    M Cd


                            .                              N
sar    5      6      1      6P     5      3      2      3G
                                    .      ...         .
pes                                6 1 6 212 66/. 6165 3
                                        ___      ____
txt                                Obahing jaman saman-tya
anl                                     M 1.3      M Cd
```

Ladrang *Pangkur*, Sléndro Pathet Manyura
(Sindhèn Cèngkok by Ki Wasitodipuro)

```
sar    3      2      3      1      3      2      1      6N
                                 __  __  __ __      __   .
pes                             .3 3.2 .212 .1 3/ 1.3 2.16
                                     ___         ___     .
txt                             Parabé Sang Mara Ba- ngun
anl                                      M 3.1        M Cb
```

117

sar	1̇	6	3	2P	5	3	2	1N
pes					.2 3.2	121 2.6	3/ 3.1	3.21
txt					Sepat	domba	kali	O - ya
anl						M 2.1		M Cf

sar	3	5	3	2P	6	5	3	2N
pes					.61.6	2.12 .6	3/3.6	.6532
txt					Aja do-lan	lan	wong	priya
anl						M 1.3		M Cb

sar	5	3	2	1P	3	2	1	N 6G
pes					.3 3.2.212	.1 3/	1.3	2.16
txt					Geng rèmèh	nora	prasa-	ja
anl						M 3.1		M Cb

Minggah

sar	.	3	.	2	.	3	.	1
pes					.23.2 1.2	.6 3/	3.1	3.21
txt					Mingkar mingkuring	hangkara		
anl						M 2.1		M Cf

Appendix 2: Pathet Manyura

```
sar     .     3     .     2     .     1     .     6N
                                                    .
pes                       .3  3.3  3.3  3 3 356 3/ 3.1 2.16//
                                                       .
txt                       Hakarana karenan mar-di si- wi

anl                                  M 4.1              M Ca


sar     1     1     .     .     6     6     1     2P
        .     .                             .
pes     6 3 .56 1               .2 3.1 212 .1 6/ 612 2

txt     Rama                    Sinawung resmining kidung

anl        M Ba                           M 2.2     M Be


sar     3     2     6     3     .     2     .     1N
        .     .
pes                             .1 2 3 .3 121 6/ .3 2.121

txt                             Sinuba sinung    karta*

anl                                       M 2.2   M or S Cf


sar     .     2     .     3     6     5     3     2P

pes                             .6 1 2.1 6/ .3 2.12

txt                             Mrih kre  -  tarta

anl                                       M 1.1   M Ch
```

---

*This word appears as "sinukarta" in other versions of this poem.

```
sar    3      2      5      3      6      5      3      2N
                                   —  .—  .—. .—        ——   ——
pes                                .6 1.6 2.1 2 .6 3/ 3536 .6532
txt                                Pakarti ning ngelmu lu - hung
anl                                        M 1.3         M Cb


              .      .      .
sar    6      1      3      2      6      3      2      1P
                                   —. .—. . .—          ——
pes                                .2 3.2 1.2.6 3/ .532 2.1
txt                                Kang tumrap nèng Tanah Jawa
anl                                        M 2.1       M Cc


                                                        N
sar    .      3      .      2      .      1      .      6G
                                                        .
                                   —  —— —— —
pes                                .3 3.2 212 .1 3/ 1.3 2.16
txt                                Agama a - geming a- ji
anl                                        M 3.1       M Cb
```

Appendix 2: Pathet Manyura

Gendhing *Perkutut Manggung*, Kethuk 2 Kerep,
Minggah Ladrang, Sléndro Pathet Manyura
(Sindhèn Cèngkok by Ki Wasitodipuro)

```
sar    .    1    1    .    1    1    2    3
                                __  . .  __  .
pes                        .5 6 1 2 / .6  16 5.3
txt                        Radèn       ra - dèn
anl                        M 1.1          M Cd


sar    5    6    5    3    2    1    2    1N
                                __
pes                        .2  3 / 6 5 3  2 .1
txt                        Ku-su- mas  -  tra
anl                        M Sh       M Ce


sar    .    1    1    .    1    1    2    3
                              __ . .    ..
pes                        .5  6 1 2 / 216 5.3
txt                        Yandhuk    yan-dhuk
anl                        M 1.1       M Ce


sar    5    6    5    3    2    1    2    1N
                           __ __ __ __      __
pes                        .3 3.2 2 12 .13/3.1 3.232 1
txt                        Careming rèh palakrama
anl                        M 3.1       M Cf
```

121

```
sar    3       5       3       2       6       3       5       6
                                       .       .       .   .   .   .
pes                                    .2      3 /     3  .1  2  .1 6//
txt                                    Go-nas  ga  -   nès
anl                                    M Sh        M Ca


                                   .
sar    3       5       6           1       6       5       2       3N
               .   __      __  .        __      .   .   .   .
pes            62  .6/ 56  .3 1//       .5  6   1  2/  2.1 6  5.3
txt            Ra- ma-né   dhéwé        Moring      gen  -  dhing
anl            M 1.2   M Bc             M 1.1       M Ce


sar    2       1       2       .       2       1       6       5
                                                       .       .
                                        __     __
pes                                    .2  3  .12/  6 216/  1.653
txt                                    Mo-ring     gen  -   dhing
anl                                            M 2.2   M P Cf  M Cc


                                                                   N
sar    3       3       .       5       6       1       2       1G
       .       .               .       .
                                __     __     __               __     __
pes                            .3     3.2    2.1   6123/ .3  5. 321
txt                            Pi-natut  lawan wi  -  rama
anl                            M 3.2               M Cd
```

122

Appendix 2: Pathet Manyura

Minggah

```
sar   3    6    3    2    5      6      5      3
                                 . .    ‾  .
pes                          .5  6 1 2/ .6 1  6 5 3
txt                              Jo-gan    Pu - ra
anl                              M 1.1      M Cd


sar   6    1    3    2    6      3      2      1N
                             ‾.  .  ‾. . .
pes                          .2  3 .3 1 2 . 6 3/ 3.1 3.2321
txt                              Patih Prabu  A-mi-ja - ya
anl                              M 2.2          M Cf


sar   3    6    3    2    5      6      5      3P
                             ‾        .  .. ‾      . .
pes                          .6 6 . 2 12 .6 6/ 2.16 5.3
txt                              Nali- kani- ra ing da-lu
anl                                   M 1.2       M Ce


sar   6    1    3    2    6      3      2      1N
                             ‾.  .  ‾. . .  ‾
pes                          .2  3 .2 1.2 .6 3/ .653 2.1
txt                          Wong Agung mangsah semè- di
anl                              M 2.1          M Ce
```

123

```
sar    3      6      3      2      6      3      5      6P
                                  ‾. .‾  . .   ...    . .   . .
pes                              .1 2 .2 2.2 6123 / 3.1 2.16
txt                               Sirep kang bala wana - ra
anl                                   M 3.2        M Ca


sar    3      5      6      1̇     5      3      5      6N
                                  ‾. . ..‾ . .         ‾
pes                              .2 3.53 .2 1.2 / .6 5 .3 6 6
txt                               Sada -  ya wus  samya gu-ling
anl                                   M 2.3         M Aa


sar    3      2      3      2      5      6      5      3P
                                  ‾  ‾. . .‾   . .
pes                              .6 6.2 1 2.6 6/2.16 5 3
txt                               Nadyan a-ri sudarsa - na
anl                                   M 1.2        M Ce

                                                          N
sar    6      1̇     3      2      6      3      2      1G
                                  ‾. . ‾. . .‾
pes                              .2 3 .2 1 2.6 3/ 3.1 3.2321
txt                               Wus dangu dènira gu- ling
anl                                   M 2.1        M Cf
```

124

Appendix 2: Pathet Manyura

Gendhing *Puspa Warna*, Sléndro Pathet Manyura
(Sindhèn Cèngkok by Ki Wasitodipuro)

```
sar    .    2    .    3    .      2      .    1N

pes                            . 2  3 / .  . .3   5 321

txt                              Ku-su      mas- tra

anl                              M Sh       M Cd



                                                      N
sar    .    3    .    2P   .      1      .    6G

pes                            .3 3.2 212 .1 3/1.3 2.16

txt                            Careming rèh palakrama

anl                                M 3.1      M Cb



sar    .    2    .    3    .      2      .    1N

pes                            . 6  1 212 16 / .3 .321

txt                               Mo-ring    gen- dhing

anl                                M 1.1      M Cf



                                                      N
sar    .    3    .    2P   .      1      .    6G

pes                            .2 3.1 2 / .6 5 3.6  6

txt                            Pinatut la-wan wira - ma

anl                                M 2.2      M Aa
```

125

Ngelik

```
sar    .    3̇    .    2̇    .    3̇    .    1̇N

pes                         . 6 1 2̇. / . .6 .653/
txt                            Kembang      kencur
anl                            M 1.1        M Cf


                                                  N
sar    .    3    .    5P   .    6    .    3G

pes    5 6 1̇              .6 6 .2 121 2.6 6/ 216 5.3
txt                      Kacaryan anggung ci-na- tur
anl      M Be                    M 1.2        M Ce


sar    .    1    .    2    .    3    .    1N

pes                      .2 3.12 .6 3/ 353 2.1
txt                      Sèdhet kang sari- ra
anl                            M 2.2     M Cd


                                                  N
sar    .    3    .    2P   .    1    .    6G

pes                      .3  3 3.56 3/ 3.1 2.16
txt                      Gandes ing wi-ra- ga
anl                            M 4.1     M Ca
```

Appendix 2: Pathet Manyura

```
sar    .    2    .    3    .       2    .       1N
                                 __   ..  __      __
pes                            .6   12  .6  3/  653  2.1
txt                            Kè- wes yèn ngandi-ka
anl                                M 1.1       M Ce


                                                    N
sar    .    3    .    2P   .       1    .       6G
                                                    .
                               __   __          __   __
pes                          .3   3  .3  56  3/  1.3  2.16
txt                          Anganga - nyut ji- wa
anl                               M 4.1      M Cb
```

Srepegan, Sléndro Pathet Manyura (Sindhèn Cèngkok by Tukinem)

```
          P         P            P            P
sar   3N  2N   3N   2N   5N   3N      5N      3N

pes1                     3    5       6    5 3/
txt1                    -Man  é   -  man éman
anl1                          M 4.1
pes2                              2    3   3 5 3
txt2                             Ra- dèn ra  -
anl2                              M 2.3
```

127

```
           P                  N           P              P
sar   2N   1N    2N          1GS    2N    1N    2N       1N

pes1   6    5    3     2  1
txt1   é    -             man
anl1         M Ce
pes2   2 /  3    2           1
txt2         dèn
anl2            M or S Cf


           P          P              P        .          N
sar   3N   2N    3N   2N      5N     6N       1N         6GS

                 .    .  .    .                .
pes              2    3 /  1   2               1          6
txt1             Ri - ris  har - da
txt2             Dre- sing kar - sa
anl              M Sh                    M Cf


      .    P    .    P              P
sar   1N   6N   1N   6N      5N     3N       5N         3N

                                .       .
pes              6    6     1    2/     6    5          3//
txt              Go - nas             ga    -          nès
anl                   M 1.1                 M Cf
```

Appendix 2: Pathet Manyura

```
                 P               N
sar    6N    5N       3N      2GS

        •     •
pes    6 1 6  2   6    3 / 212 2

txt1   Hardaning wong lumak-sa- na

txt2   Mamayu ha- yu ning Pra-ja

anl         M 1.3         M Ch
```

Ketawang *Suksma Ilang*, Sléndro Pathet Manyura
(Sindhèn Cèngkok by Tukinem)

```
sar    •     •      2      6      1      2      3      2N
                           •

pes                                      2   3 / 3212 2

txt                                      Ri-ris har- da

anl                                      M Sh    M Ch
```

```
                                                        N
sar    6     1      2      3P     6      5      3      2G
       •
                                  •      •
pes                               6  1  6  2  6 3/ 3212 1//

txt                               Hardaning wong lumaksa-na

anl                                       M 1.3        M Ch
```

129

```
sar     3       3       .       .       3       3       5       3N
                                                        ..
pes     1 216/ 123                              5 612/ 653   3//
              .
txt     Rama                                    Dresing kar- sa

anl     M Cf  M Be                              M 1.1   M Cf


                .       ...     ..      .       ...     .
sar     6       1       6       5P      1       6       5       N
                                                                3G
pes             1 123/ 16165 5//        6 6 212 6 6/ 61653 3

txt             Gonas   ga -   nès      Mamayu hayu-ning Pra-ja

anl             M Sh    M Cf            M 1.2   M Cd
```

Ngelik

```
                                                        .
sar     .       .       3       5       6       .       1       6N
                                        .   .   . ..
pes                                     2   3   2 12/ 6 5 36 6
                                            —           —
txt                                     Midering rat angalangut

anl                                     M 2.1       M Aa


                                        .       .       .       N
sar     3       5       6       1P      3       2       1       6G
                                        .   .   . ..
pes                                     2   3   2 12/ 6 6.653/
                                            —       —
txt                                     Lala-na ja-jah ne -

anl                                     M 2.1       M P Cf
```

130

Appendix 2: Pathet Manyura

```
               .       .                     .       .       .
sar            1       1       .       .     3       2       1       6N

                       . .                         .   . ..
pes    3 5 6 1 1                                 2 3 2 12/ 6 65 36 6
                   ‾‾‾
txt    ga  -  ri                            Mubeng tepi ning samo-dra

anl        M Ba                                  M 2.1       M Aa


                                   .       .       .       .       N
sar    3       5       6       1P  3       2       1       6G

                                               .   . . ..          . . .
pes1                                         2 3 2 12/ 6  6/ 61216
                                                   ‾‾          ‾‾‾‾
txt1                                         Sumengka hanggraning wu-

anl1                                             M 2.1     M P   M Ce

                                               .   . . ..          .
pes2                                         2 3 2 12/ 6  6/ 6 16
                                                   ‾‾
txt2                                         Sumengka hanggraning wu-

anl2                                             M 2.1     M P   M Cd


sar    3       3       .       .     6       5       3       2N

                                           .       .
pes1   5 3                           6 1 6 2 6 3/ 53 6532
       ‾‾‾                                      ‾‾ ‾‾‾
txt1   kir                           A-na-lasak wana wa-sa

pes2   5 3
       ‾‾‾
txt2   kir

anl                                        M 1.3       M Cd
```

131

```
                                                                    N
sar     6       1       2       3P      6       5       3       2G
        .
pes1                                    .       .
                                    6   1   6   2   6   3/  3212  2
                                                           ————
txt1                                Tumurun ing jurang tre - bis

anl1                                    M 1.3           M Ch

pes2                                3   3   2   2   1   3/  5332  2
                                                           ————
txt2                                Tumurun ing jurang tre - bis

anl2                                    M 3.1           M Cf
```

Ketawang *Suksma Ilang*, Sléndro Pathet Manyura
(Sindhèn Cèngkok by Ki Wasitodipuro)

```
sar     .       .       2       6       1       2       3       2N
                                .
                                        ——              ——  ——
pes                                     .2  3 /     3.5 3.2  2
                                                    —————————
txt                                     Ku - su     mas  -  tra

anl                                         M Sh        M Cf


                                                                    N
sar     6       1       2       3P      6       5       3       2G
        .
                                        —.—  .—. .——    ——  ——
pes                                     .61.6 2.1 2. 6 3/3.6 532//
                                        —————         ———
txt                                 Careming rèh pala kra-ma

anl                                         M 1.3       M Cb
```

132

Appendix 2: *Pathet Manyura*

```
sar     3       3       .       .       3       3       5       3N

pes     2   6.12 3//                        .5  6.12 / 6 .165 3//

txt     Ra-ma                               Mo-ring   gen - dhing

anl       M Ba                              M 1.1     M Cd



sar     6       1       6       5P      1       6       5       3G (N)

pes         .1 1.23/ 1  2165 5//    .6 6.2 12 .6 6/ 2.16 5.3

txt             Gonas  ga -  nès    Pinatut lawan wira - ma

anl             M Sh    M Cd            M 1.2       M Ce
```

Ngelik

```
sar     .       .       3       5       6       .       1       6N

pes                                     .1 2.2 212/ .3 1 1216 6

txt                                     Midering rat angala- ngut

anl                                         ?           M Ca



sar     3       5       6       1P      3       2       1       6G (N)

pes                                     .2 3.5 3 .2 12/ .6 5 3.6 6//

txt                                     Lala - na jajah nega- ri

anl                                     M 2.3       M Aa
```

133

```
sar   1       1      .      .      3      2      1      6N
pes  6 3.56 1                     .2   3.1  2/ .6  5  3.6 6
txt  Rama                          Mubeng tepining samo- dra
anl    M Ba                           M 2.2        M Aa


sar   3       5      6      1P     3      2      1      N
                                                       6G
pes                              .2  3.5 3.2 1.2/.6  5  3.6 6//
txt                               Sumengka hanggraning wukir
anl                                    M 2.3       M Aa


sar   3       3      .      .      6      5      3      2N
pes  6153 3                       .6  6.5 5.3 6/ 3.6 5.32
txt  Yan- dhuk                    Analasak wana wa-sa
anl  M Cd                              M 3.1       M Cb


sar   6       1      2      3P     6      5      3      N
                                                       2G
pes                              .6  1.6 2.1 2.6 3/ 212 2
txt                               Tumurun ing jurang tre-bis
anl                                    M 1.3       M Ch
```

134

Appendix 2: Pathet Manyura

Ladrang *Wilujeng*, Sléndro Pathet Manyura (Sindhèn Cèngkok by Gitosaprodjo)

sar	2	1	2	3	2	1	2	6N

sar	3	3	.	.P	6	5	3	2N
pes						6 1216/	.3	212//
txt						Trahing	na-	ta
anl						M 1.1		M Ch

sar	5	6	5	3P	2	1	2	6N
pes		6 1 2/	. 6165	53//		3 3 2 2 1 3/.31	21	6//
txt		Ya mas	ya mas,		Garwa risang	Danan	Jaya
anl		M 1.1	M Cd			M 3.1		M Ca

sar	2	1	2	3P	2	1	2	N 6G
pes					2 2 2 2 2 2 3 12/.6	5 . 36	6
txt				Dèn prayitna	Sabarang haywa	sembrana
anl					M 2.2		M Aa

Ngelik

```
                                    .               .
sar    .      .      6      .      1      5      1      6N
                                   ... ..
pes                               232 12/ . 6 5 . 36 6
                                              ‒          ‒
txt                               Parabé Sang Mara Bangun
anl                                 M 2.1       M Aa


                            .
sar    3      5      6      1P     6      5      3      2N
                                   .      ...
pes                               6 1 6 212. 6 3/. 212 2
                                                ‒      ‒
txt                               Sepat domba Kali  O - ya
anl                                      M 1.3      M Ch


                                    .              .
sar    6      6      .      .P     1      5      1      6N
                                  . . ...
pes                               2 3 212/ . 6 5. 36 6/ 5
                                         ‒          ‒   ‒
txt                               Aja dolan lan wong priya
anl                                  M 2.1    M P Aa


       .      .                                         .
sar    1      1      3      2P     .      1      2      6G
                                                        .
       .
pes    3 5 6 1                    3 3 2 2 1 3/ .1 3 216
       ‒‒‒‒‒‒‒                               ‒‒   ‒‒‒.
txt                               Guramèh nora prasa-ja
anl         M Ba                         M 3.1     M Cb
```

Appendix 2: Pathet Manyura

Umpak

```
sar    2      1      2      3      2      1      2      6N
                                                        .
pes                                 2  3 /  .  3 1   216//
                                              ‾‾‾      .
txt                                 Jarwa      mu - dha
anl                                 M Sh       M Ca


sar    3      3      .      .P     6      5      3      2N
                                        .     ...
pes      1  2  1  6/ 1  2  3//    6 1 6  212 6  3/. 212 2//
                  .
txt      Go-nès                  Mudhané Sang Prabu Kres-na
anl          M Cf       M Be         M 1.3       M Ch


sar    5      6      5      3P     2      1      2      6N
                     .                                  .
pes      5  6/     6165 5  3//       2  3/  .  3 1   216//
                                              ‾‾      .
txt      Ya mas   ya    mas        Pupung   a - nom
anl      M Sh     M Cd              M Sh     M Ca


                                                        N
sar    2      1      2      3P     2      1      2      6G
                                    . . . . ..
pes        6 1 2 . 3  3//         2 3 2 12/ .6 5 . 36 6
               .                           ‾‾          ‾‾
txt        Ramané dhéwé           Ngudi sarananing Praja
anl            M Ba                M 2.1       M Aa
```

Mode in Javanese Music

Ngelik

```
sar    .     .     6     .     1̇     5     1̇     6N
pes                            2 353 212/.6 5 . 36 6
txt                            Garwa Sang Sindura Prabu
anl                              M 2.3      M Aa


sar    3     5     6     1̇P    6     5     3     2N
pes                            6 1 6 212.6  3/ .12 2
txt                            Wicara mawa ka - ra-na
anl                                M 1.3      M Bf


sar    6     6     .     .P    1̇     5     1̇     6N
pes                            2 3 1 2/ 6 5.3 6   6/ 5
txt                            Aja dolan lan wani - ta
anl                              M 2.2    M P Aa


sar    1̇     1̇     3     2P    .     1     2     6G
pes    3 5 6 1̇                 3 3 2 2 1 3/.1 3  216
txt                            Tan nyata asring katarka
anl       M Ba                     M 3.1      M Cb
```

138

APPENDIX 3

GENDHING IN SLÉNDRO SANGA
WITH SINDHÈN NOTATION

Ayak-ayakan, Sléndro Pathet Sanga (Sindhèn Cèngkok by Tukinem)

```
                                                        .N
sar                                                     1G


            .               .N              .           .N
sar    .    2N      .       1P      .       2N     .    1P


            .               .N                          N
sar    .    3N      .       2P      .       6N     .    5GS
                                .       .           .
pes                             1       2  /  6     1 6  5 5//
txt                             Wi  -  ting   kla    -    pa
anl                               S Sh            S Cf
```

```
                              N                           N
sar    1̇      6N     5      6P      5       3N      5     6P

pes                         5    3 /  2     3       5    6//
                            _____
txt                         Ra   -    ma

anl                           S Sh              S Ba


                              N                           N
sar    5      3N     5      6P      3       5N      6     5GS

pes                         1̇  2̇  1̇  6̇  1̇/ 5   3 25  5//
                                    ___        __
txt                         Ka- la- pa kang  ma-sih mu-dha

anl                              S 2.1          S Aa


                              N                           N
sar   [:3     2N     3      5P      3       2N      3     5P

pes          2 / 3 2 1 2 3 5                        5  5  6
                 _____                             ___
txt          Ra- ma                                 Ya mas

anl    S Sh       S Ba                                 S Be


       .                      N                           N
sar    1      6N     5      6P      5       3N      2     1GS

pes    1̇//                  1̇   2̇ 1̇  6̇ 1̇   5  2/ 3 2 1 1//
       _                                              ___
txt1                        Sa -  lu-gu- né   Sa-lu- gu   né

txt2                        Dre-sing kar-sa   Dresing kar- sa

anl2                               S 2.1        M or S Cf
```

Appendix 3: Pathet Sanga

```
                              N                          N
sar    2      3N     2       1P      2      3N      2    1P
pes      1   2/  3   2    1 1//              1   2  1 6  1/
txt      Ra- dèn ra    -      dèn            Sa-lu-gu - né
anl    S Sh         S Cf                         S 2.1


                              N                          N
sar    3      2N     1       2P      5      6N      1    6GS
pes      6  5/ 6   1    2//      5    6  1  5  2/ 1 1612 16 6//
txt                          Wong mar - di pikir ra- harja
anl    S P Cg      S Be               S 1.1             S Cf


                              N                          N
sar    5      3N     5       6P      5      3N      5    6P
pes      1    2/ 3 2 1 6    6//                  2  2  2  2
txt      Ra - ma ra  -    ma                     Riris harda
anl        S Sh       S Cc


                              N                          N
sar    2      3N     2       1P      6      5N      3    5GS
pes    2 2 1 6 1 5 2/ 321 1//        2  2/  2 6  2 1 6 5//
txt    Hardaning wong lumaksana      Dresing kar-sa
anl      S 2.1          S Cf         S Sh      S Cb
```

Mode in Javanese Music

```
                                N                               N
sar    3        2N      3       5P      3        2N     3        5P
       .        .       .       .       .        .      .        .

pes         1      2/   2 6  216 5//              2  2/  2 6   2
                       ‾‾‾    · · ·                    ‾‾‾    ‾
                        ·                              ·
txt         Ra  -   dèn ra- dèn              Dresing kar- sa

anl         S  Sh      S  Cb                      S Sh   S P Cb



                                N                               N
sar    3        2N      1       2P      3        5N    6        5GS:]
                                .                 .    .        .

pes    1  6  5/ 6  1  2//         1  2  1  6 1/ 5  3  25  5//
       ‾‾‾‾‾‾‾‾‾‾‾‾‾‾‾‾‾         .  .  .  .‾    .      .‾
          ·       ·                        ·          ·
txt                               Ma- ma-yu ha-yuning Pra-ja

anl              S  Be                 S 2.1         S Aa


Suwuk:*


                           N                                N
sar    2        3N      2  1P      3        5N    6          5G
                                   .         .    .          .

pes         2  2  2  2  2  2  1  1  6  2/  6 2   1 6 5
                                    ·      ‾‾‾   ‾‾‾‾
                                    ·      · ·   · ·
txt         Dresing karsa Ma-ma-yu ha-yuning Pra- ja

anl                    S 3.1                 S Cb
```

_____

*This suwuk is played after the gatra 5321GS in this recording. The second poetic line written beneath that gatra is sung only before the suwuk. If the gendhing is repeated as indicated by the brackets, the text will have to be changed to preserve the integrity of the wangsalan.

Appendix 3: Pathet Sanga

Ladrang *Clunthang*, Sléndro Pathet Sanga
(Sindhèn Cèngkok by Kenang Darmoredjono)

```
sar    .    5    .    6    .    2    .    1N

pes                        1 2 6 1 5 2/.3 532321

txt                        Parabé Sang Mara Bangun

anl                              S 2.2      S Cd


sar    .    5    .    6P   .    1    .    6N

pes                        1 2 6 1/ 5 532/ 235 6

txt                        Sepat domba kali  O - ya

anl                              S 2.2   S Cf  S Ba


sar    .    5    .    6P   .    3    .    5N

pes                        1 2 6 1/ 5 3 . 2 5 5

txt                        Aja dolan lan wong priya

anl                              S 2.2      S Aa


                                             N
sar    .    2    .    1P   .    6    .    5G

pes                        2 2 1 161.62/6 16165

txt                        Geramèh no- ra prasaja

anl                              S 3.1      S Cf
```

143

```
sar      .      1      .      6      .      3      .      5N
                                 .             .             .

pes                  2 3 21 6//          1  2/ 6   2  16165//
                     ‾‾‾‾‾‾ .            .             . . ..
txt                  Ra  -  ma            Su-ku pal-wa

anl                      S Cd             S Sh      S Cb



sar      .      1      .      6P     .      3      .      5N
                                 .             .             .

pes          2 3 5 3 2/ 2   321 6//     2 2 1 161 6 2/ 6 16165
                        ‾‾‾‾‾‾ .             . . .. . .   . . ..
txt      -Man éman éman é  -  man,    Palwa kandheg ing samodra

anl          S 4.1     S Cd                 S 3.1      S Cf



sar      .      1      .      6P     .      3      .      5N
                                 .             .             .

pes                  2 3 21 6//           1  2/  6  2  16165//
                     ‾‾‾‾‾‾ .            .              . . ..
txt                  Ra  -  ma            Solah  ba-wa

anl                      S Cd             S Sh      S Cb


                                                          N
sar      .      2      .      3P     .      2      .      1G
                                 .             .

pes      6165/612//    5 3/ 2123//    5 6 5 1 5 2/ .3 532321
         . . .. .
txt      Rama,        É ramané dhéwé, Labuh labet marang Praja

anl      S Cf  S Be   S Sh  S Bb          S 1.3        S Cd*
```

---

*Usually the first time the first gongan is sung in this piece, the
pesindhèn sings alone, using wangsalan. Upon repetition of this gongan after
the second gongan, both gérong and pesindhèn sing.

Appendix 3: Pathet Sanga

Gendhing *Gambir Sawit*, Kethuk 2, Minggah Kethuk 4,
Sléndro Pathet Sanga (Sindhèn Cèngkok by Ki Wasitodipuro)

sar	.	3	5	2	.	3	5	6

sar	2	2	.	.	2	3	2	1N

sar	.	.	.	3	2	1	2	6

sar	2	2	.	.	2	3	2	1N
pes					1	2/ .	.3 212	1
txt					Ri- ris		har - da	
anl					S Sh		M or S Cf	

sar	.	.	3	2	.	1	6	5
pes					1	2/ .	2 . 6	1
txt					Ri-ris		har - da	
anl					S Sh		S Ca	

145

```
                              .
sar    .      .      5     6   1     6     5     3N
                              . . .   ___     __ __
pes  6 5                      1 2. 1 61/ .5 5/ 535 6.5
       ‾                                       ‾‾‾
txt                          Hardaning wong lumaksa -

anl                          S 2.1    S P   S Cd


sar    2      2      .     3   5     3     2     1
                                   == ==        __
pes  3.2//                     5  656 .16 5/ .2 1
       ‾                                       _
txt  na                       Dresing       karsa

anl                                S 1.1     S Ch

                                                    N
sar    3      5      3     2   .     1     6      5G
                                  == == ==   __    .
pes  6 1//                     2  2.2 2.2 2.1 161.6 2/2.6 1.65//
     ._                                   ._  .    ._   .._
txt                           Dresing karsa Mamayu hayuning Praja

anl                                S 3.1              S Ca


sar    .      .      .     5   2     3     5     6
                          .    .     .     .     .
pes        .1   2/  . 3 21 .165//       .1  2/.3216/
           __         __  .._           __    .
txt       Ya  mas   ya - mas          Nata dé -

anl       S Sh      S Ce             S Sh   M or S P Cc
```

Appendix 3: Pathet Sanga

```
sar    2     2      .     .      2      3      2      1N

pes  6.12//                    .5 6.5 161 .5 2/ 2 1.61

txt  wa                        Jrudemungé ngela e   -

anl  S Be                             S 1.3      S Ch


sar    .     .      3     2      .      1      2      6

pes    1                       2 2.1 1.6.165.612/.2 3.216/

txt    la                      Kawilet langlangan   lalu

anl                                   S 3.2      S P Cd


sar    2     2      .     .      2      3      2      1N

pes  1 2//                      1 2 165 5.61.5 2/2.5 .5321

txt                            Lengleng kalingan kalunglun

anl  M or S Bf                        S 2.1      S Cb


sar    .     .      3     2      .      1      6      5

pes                             1 2 .6 1/ .5  3  2.5 5

txt                            Kalangen langening branta

anl                                   S 2.2      S Aa
```

147

```
sar     .       .       5       6       1       6       5       3N
                                        ·
pes                                     5 5.1 61 .5 5/ 561.65/ 6
txt                                     Ngarang mirong rangu ra- ngu
anl                                         S 1.2      S P Cf


sar     2       2       .       3       5       3       2       1
pes 5.3.2//                             1 2.3 2.1 61.52/2    1.61
txt                                     Karungrungan mangiri -
anl M or S Cc                               S 2.3        S Ch


                                                                N
sar     3       5       3       2       .       1       6       5G
pes     1                               1 2 .1 61/ .5 5.32/2.35.6
txt     ya                              Riyaning tyas lir ti-nu -
anl                                         S 2.1     S Cf    S Ba


Ngelik

sar     6       6       .       .       6       6       .       .
pes     6                               6       1       . 1 6 5/
txt     tus                             Go - nès
anl                                             S P Cf
```

Appendix 3: Pathet Sanga

```
sar    2     2              .     2     3     2     1N

pes   612                         1 2.6  161 . 6.165/ .5 6.561/

txt                               Puspa kresna ing As-tana

anl  M or S Be                         S 2.2         S Bb



sar    .     .    3    2     .     1     2     6

pes                               2 2.1 161 .6 2/ 2.6 1.6 5/

txt                               Kalabang sinandhung mu-rub

anl                                    S 3.1       S P Ca



sar    2     2    .    .     2     3     2     1N

pes  6.1.2                         1 2 .6 161 .6 5/ .5 5.61

txt                               Karenan ma-rang sihi-pun

anl  M or S Be                         S 2.2       S Be



sar    .     .    3    2     .     1     6     5

pes                               1 2.3  2.161/53 2.5  5

txt                               Satri-ya andeling yu-da

anl                                    S 2.3     S Aa
```

149

```
sar    .     .      5    6    1    6    5    3N
                                  .
                              .─  .─       .
                              ─   ─        ──
pes                          5 5.1 61 .5 5/ 5616 5/
                                         ─
txt                          Surasaning tyas wula -
anl                              S 1.2      S P Cf


sar    2     2      .    3    5    3    2    1
                                  . . ─    .─
                                      ─    ─
pes 6.53 2                   1 2 165 5.61.5 2/ 21.61
    ─────                         ──  ──       .
txt ngun                     Wilatung buntal sa-ro-
anl M or S Cc                     S 2.1      S Ch


                                              N
sar    3     5      3    2    .    1    6    5G
                                       .      .
                                   ─
pes    1                     2 2.1 161 .6 2/ 2.6 1.65
                                   .   .      .   ..
txt    tan                   Anggung katingal wong a-gung
anl                               S 3.1      S Ca


sar    .     .      .    5    2    3    5    6
                             .    .    .    .
       ─          ══   ══
pes    .1   2/  . _ 3 21 .165//    1 2/ . .3 2 1.6/
                        ..                        .
txt      Ya  mas  ya  mas,      Na-ta  dé -
anl      S Sh     S Ce          S Sh   M or S P Cc
```

Appendix 3: Pathet Sanga

```
sar    2      2       .         .      2      3      2      1N

pes .12                                1 212 .1 61 .5 2/3.212 1
txt                                    Kunta-né Sri Danarda  - na
anl M or S Bf                             S 2.1       M or S Cf


sar    .      .       3         2      .      1      2      6

pes                                           1   2/ . . 321 . 6/
txt                                           Jroning  nén - dra
anl                                           S Sh   M or S P Cc


sar    2      2       .         .      2      3      2      1N

pes .12//     2       2  .1  161  .6   2 /   3 2.1  1
txt           Ka  -  cak-ra ba  -  wa  mung - si  - ra
anl M or S Bf             S 3.1              S Cf


sar    .      2       .         1      .      6      .      5

pes                                    1  2 / . 3. 2 1 6.5
txt                                    Ya mas    ya   mas
anl                                    S Sh      S Ce
```

```
sar    .    6    .    5    .    3    .    2N
                                      ‾    ‾‾
pes                        .3  5/ . . 653 2  2//
txt                        Jro-ning   nén - dra
anl                        S Sh       S Cc


sar    .    3    .    5    .    2    .    1
                        ‾‾ ‾‾       ‾‾ •‾‾
pes                     .2 25 5//   5 6 1 .5 2/3 2 1  1
                        ‾
txt                     Ya ra- ma,  -Man éman éman é - man
anl                        S Aa        S 1.1    S Cf


sar    .    2    .    1    .    6    .    N
                                      •        5G
                     ‾ ‾‾ ‾‾ ‾‾ ‾‾              •
pes                  .2 2.2 2.2 2.1 161.62/3.2.1 6.5//
                                    •• •   ‾‾‾  ••
txt                  Jroning néndra Kacakra bawa mungsira
anl                          S 3.1          S Ce


Minggah

sar    .    .    .    6    .    .    .    5
                          •                    •
pes    .1 2/ .  2 .32 1.6//  2 2.1 1 61 .6 2/ 2.6 1
                ‾‾‾   •                •     ‾‾  ••
txt    Basa     pur - wa    Lalu diwa-saning sur-ya
anl    S Sh  S Cd           S 3.1        S Ca
```

Appendix 3: Pathet Sanga

```
sar    .      .       .      1      .      .      .      6

pes  6 5//      1    . 6 5 6.1//.5  61 .5 2.1 561 2/2.32 1.6//

txt             Ya       mas,  Ya mu-lané Ya mu - la - né

anl                S Bb            S 1.1           S Cd


sar    .      .       .      1      .      .      .      6

pes    5 51 .5 2/.161 51 1//   .1  2/ .  2 .321  6//

txt    Gonas ganès wicara- né    Ya mu - la - né

anl      S 1.2      S Bd       S Sh    S Cd


sar    .      .       .      2      .      .      .      1N

pes  .6 1.65/612//          1 2.3 2.1 61.52/ 2.5 3.21//

txt  Ya mas                 A-ja gingsiring prasetya

anl  S Cf  S Be                 S 2.3      S Cb


sar    .      .       .      2      .      .      .      1

pes    5 .6 161 .2 3 2//     5  6 1.16 5/ .2 161

txt    Kancané dhéwé         Peksi       raja

anl          S Ba            S 1.1     S Ch
```

153

```
sar    .        .        .     2        .        .        .     6
                                                                 .
pes                                 1 2.32 .1 61.52/2.32 1.6//
txt                                 Pamba- baring guna bisa
anl                                          S 2.3      S Cd


sar    .        .        .     1        .        .        .     6
                                                                 .
pes     2 61 .5  2/32.1 1//161 1.2 2//.1 2/  2.3 2  1.6//
txt     Ya ra-ma-né dhé-wé, -Man éman,  Denta be - ri
anl        S 2.2     S Cf    S Be   S Sh   S Cd


sar    .        .        .     2        .        .        .    1N
pes     .6 1.6 5/61 2            .1  2.1  61. 5 2/.321 1//
txt       Gonès                  Anga-wruhi barang karya
anl        S Cf  S Be                S 2.1     S Cf


sar    .        .        .     2        .        .        .    1
pes  .1 1235.1/5  6  161.2 32//    56 1. 5 2/. 32.1 1//
txt  Ya ra-ma ra-ma-né dhéwé      -Man éman éman é - man
anl     ?          S Ba              S 1.1     S Cf
```

Appendix 3: Pathet Sanga

```
sar    .      .      .      6      .      .      .      5

pes  .5 51 .5  2/ 5  35  .2  6//   . 1 2.1  61/ .5 3 .2 5 5//

txt  Gonas ganès wi-ca - ra-né,    Angawruhi barang kar-ya

anl     S 1.2         S Bc         S 2.1         S Aa


sar    .      .      .      1      .      .      .      6

pes  .5  5   6   1               1 2.32.16.1/.55.3.2/2.3.5.6

txt  Ra-ma                       Nali - kani-raing   da -

anl     S Be                     S 2.3     S Cf     S Ba


sar    .      .      .      3      .      .      .      2N

pes  6                            5 5.1 61 .5 5/ 5.6.1.6 5/

txt  lu                          Wong agung mangsah semè -

anl                                  S 1.2      S P Cf


sar    .      .      .      6      .      .      .      5

pes  3.2.3.5.6//                  1 2.6 1/   .5 3 2.5  5

txt  di                          Sirep kang bala wana - ra

anl     S Ba                     S 2.2         S Aa
```

sar   .   .   .   2   .   .   .   1

pes   1   2 .165 561 .5 2/ 2.1.6 1

txt   Sada- ya wus samya gu -

anl   S 2.1   S Ch

sar   .   .   .   2   .   .   .   1

pes   1   5 6.5 1.61 .5 2/ 2.5 .5321

txt   ling   Nadyan ari   sudarsa - na

anl   S 1.3   S Cb

sar   .   .   .   6   .   .   .   N / 5G

pes   2 2.1 161 .6 2/ 3.2.1 6.5

txt   Wus dangu dè - nira gu - ling

anl   S 3.1   S Ce

Ketawang *Kasatriyan*, Sléndro Pathet Sanga
(Sindhèn Cèngkok by Prawotosaputro)

sar   1   2   1   6   3   2   6   5N

pes   .1 2/ .6 2 1 .6 5

txt   Ri- ris harda

anl   S Sh   S Cb

Appendix 3: Pathet Sanga

```
                                                                      N
sar   1       2       1       6P      2       1       6       5G
                                      ___ ___ ___ ___
pes                                   .2 2 1 1 6 2/6 2 1 .6 5//
txt                                   Hardaning wong lumaksana
anl                                   S 3.1        S Cb


sar   1       2       1       6       3       2       6       5N
           __      __ __ __         __      __ __ __
pes      .1  2 / .2 32 321 6//      .1  2 / .6 2 1 .6 5//
txt        Ra-ma   rama             Dresing karsa
anl        S Sh       S Cd          S Sh       S Cb


                                                                      N
sar   1       2       1       6P      2       1       6       5G
          __      __ __ __          __ __ __ __ __ __
pes     2 3 5/ 32 32 32 1 6//     .1 2 1 61/ .5 .3 25  5
txt    -Man éman é- man            Mamayu hayu ning Praja
anl      S Sh       S Cc            S 2.1        S Aa


Ngelik


             .       .       .       .
sar   6       5       2       1       3       2       6       5N
                                    __ __ __ __ __ __
pes                                 .1 2 1 61/ .5 .3 25  5
txt                                 Midering rat  angalangut
anl                                 S 2.1        S Aa
```

157

```
sar    .      .  1  6  5  2P     .        1        6      N
                                                         5G

pes                             .2  21  16  2/6  21  .6  5

txt                             Lalana  jajah  negari

anl                                  S 3.1        S Cb



sar    6      5      2      1      3        2        6     5N

pes                             .1  2  1  61/  .5  .3  25  5

txt                             Mubeng  tepi-ning  samodra

anl                                  S 2.1        S Aa



sar    .      .  1  6  5  2P     .        1        6      N
                                                         5G

pes                             .2  21  16  2 /  61  65  /6

txt                             Sumengka  hanggraning  wu-kir

anl                                  S 3.1     S P Cf



sar    1      1      2      1      3        2        1     6N

pes    . 1                       .5  61  .5  2  5  3  2/32  321  6

txt                             A-na-lasak  wana  wasa

anl    S Bf                           S 1.1            S Cc
```

Appendix 3: Pathet Sanga

```
sar      3       5       3       2P      1       6       3       5G
                                  ‾       ‾       ·       ·       ·
                                          ‾    ‾ ‾     ‾
pes                               .2 2 2 2  232 2 /.6  21 .6  5
                                             ·         · ·
txt                               Tumurun ing jurang trebis

anl                                       S Sh          S Cb
```

Gendhing *Renyep*, Kethuk 2 Kerep, Minggah Ladrang *Éling-éling Kasmaran*,
Sléndro Pathet Sanga (Sindhèn Cèngkok by Ki Wasitodipuro)

```
sar      .       .       .       2       5       3       2       1


sar      .       6       5       .       5       6       1       2N
                 ·       ·               ·


sar      .       .       .       2       5       3       2       1


sar      .       6       5       .       5       6       1       2N
                 ·       ·               ·       ·
                                         ‾    ‾ ‾   ·   ‾     ‾
pes                                      .5 5.56 1̶ 5.3̶ 2.1̶.2  3̶.1̶2
                                                     ‾    ‾       ‾
txt                                      Bayem harda Bayem harda

anl                                           Barang Miring
```

159

sar	.	3	6	5	.	.	5	.
pes							.5 5 6 .1 1	
txt							Gonès	
anl							S Be	

sar	5	5	.	6	1̇	6	5	6N
pes					2 2.2 3̸5 2.1̸		6̸.5.6̸1̸.6̸1̸56̸	
txt					Hardaning ngrasuk busana			
anl					Barang Miring			

sar	.	.	5	1̇	5	3	2	1
pes					.5 6 .1 6 5/		.2 1.6 1//	
txt					Mari		anteng	
anl					S 1.1		S Ch	

sar	.	6̣	5̣	.	5̣	6̣	1	2G (N)
pes	3̸2 . 1̸		6̸ 56̸5		.5 5 .56 1̸ 5.3̸ 2.1̸ .2 3.23̸1̸2			
txt	Ra - ma				Besu-sé saya ka- tara			
anl	Barang Miring				Barang Miring			

160

Appendix 3: Pathet Sanga

```
sar   .      .        .      2     5      3      2      1
                                       ‾      .         ‾
pes                                  .5 6 1.6  5/  .2  1.61
                                                         .
txt                                  Radèn          ra-dèn
anl                                       S 1.1      S Ch


sar   .      6        5      .     5      6      1      2N
                                   .      .      ‾      ‾
pes   ʒ2  .  ʏ    ɓ 5ɓ5      .5 5 .56 ʏ 5.ʒ 2.ʏ .2 ʒ.ʏ2
                    . ...
txt   Ra   -   M ma          Kolik priya Kolik priya
anl       Barang Miring             Barang Miring


sar   .      .        .      2     5      3      2      1
                                       ‾      .         ‾
pes                                  .5 6 1.6  5/  .2  1.61
                                                         .
txt                                  Kolik          pri-ya
anl                                       S 1.1      S Ch


sar   .      6        5      .     5      6      1      2N
                                   .      ‾    .  ‾
pes   ʒ2  .  ʏ    ɓ 5ɓ5      .5 5 .56 ʏ 5.ʒ 2.ʏ .2 ʒ.ʏ2
                    . ...
txt   Ra   -   ma            Wana-ra  Anjani  putra
anl       Barang Miring             Barang Miring
```

161

```
sar      .      3      6      5      .          .          5          .
                                                            ‾‾
pes  1̶ 2                                        .5      5  .6  1
                                                            ‾‾    .
txt                                            Go- nès
anl                                             S Be


                                              .
sar      5      5      .      6      1      6          5          6N
                                            ‾‾              ‾‾ ‾
pes                                         . . ‾.  .. . .  ‾ ‾  .
                                          2 2 .2 3̶5 2.1̶ 6̶.5 .6̶ 1
txt                                       Tuhu é - man Tuhu é-man
                                              ‾‾          ‾‾    ‾
anl                                         Barang Miring


                                       .
sar      .      .      5      1      5      3          2          1
                                          ‾        ‾.‾  .  ‾‾  ‾
pes  6̶1̶5̶6̶                               .5  6 1.6 2.165/.21.61
                                                                   .
txt                                       Tu- hu             éman
anl                                              S 1.1       S Ch


                                                                   N
sar      .      6      5      .      5      6          1          2G
         •      •                    •      •
                                     ‾ ‾‾    .. ‾‾    .        ‾‾
pes                              .5 5.5 61̶.1̶ 656 1̶ 5.3̶2.1̶.2 3̶23̶1̶2
txt                              Tuhu éman wong anom wedi ing karya
                                                                 ‾‾
anl                                       Barang Miring
```

162

Appendix 3: Pathet Sanga

Ngelik[*]

```
                                          .      .N
sar    .    6    5    .    5    6    2    1G

                          . .  ‾‾   . . ‾‾      ‾‾      .
pes                       .1 2 .6  161 .6  5/ .5  6.561

txt                       Wong anom we- di ing karya

anl                            S 2.2          S Bb



       .    .    .         .    .    .    .
sar    .    1    1    .    1    1    2    1

                              .    .
pes                          .1   2/  .  5 .5  6.1

txt                          Go-nès      go- nès

anl                          S Sh     S Be



       .    .    .    .         .
sar    3    2    1    2    .    1    6    5N

                              .    . .    .
pes                          .1 2 .3  2/ 2.6 1.65//

txt                          Yaksa    dé- wa

anl                          S 2.3       S Ca
```

---

[*]Before the ngelik, the two gatra

```
                    .  .
.  6  5  .  and  5  6  2  1
```

are played instead of

```
.  6  5  .  and  5  6  1  2
   .  .           .  .
```

163

```
sar    .      6      2̇      1̇      .      .      1̇      .

pes         .5  5̄   . 6   . 1̇
txt         Ra-ma
anl                 S Be


sar    3̇     2̇      1̇      2̇      .      1̇      6      5N

pes                             2 2.1 161 .6  2/ 2.6 1.65//
txt                             Déwa déwi lir da-na- wa
anl                               S 3.1      S Ca


sar    .      6      2̇      1̇      .      .      1̇      .

pes         1̇ 2/  . 5  .5̄ 6.1̇
txt         Go-nas       go-nès
anl         S Sh      S Be


sar    3̇     2̇      1̇      2̇      .      1̇      2̇      6N

pes                             2 2 2̇35 2 .1̇ 6.5 .6 1̇61̇56
txt                             Kala mu-dha Kala  mudha
anl                                 Barang Miring
```

Appendix 3: Pathet Sanga

```
                              .
sar    .       .      5      1      5      3       2        1

              ___           . .          ___  .─ . ── ──
pes          .5    5    .1  1//        .5 61.6  2.165/.2  1.61
                                                            .
txt                 Ya ra  -  ma        Kala          mudha

anl                    S Bd                 S 1.1      S Ch



                                                            N
sar    .       6      5      .      5      6       1        2G

                                  ___ ── . . ── . ──       ══
pes       32  .  1    6 565    .5 5.5 61.1 656 1 5.32.1.232312
                       . ...
txt       Ra   -   ma,  Kala mudha Bangkit ambèngkas durgama

anl    Barang Miring              Barang Miring



sar    .       .       .      2      5      3       2        1

                                           ___  .      ___
pes                                 .5 6 1.6 5/  .2  1.61
                                                       .
txt                                 Radèn        ra-dèn

anl                                     S 1.1      S Ch



sar    .       6      5      .      5      6       1        2N

                                            .
pes                                 3   561 5  . 3   2.12
                                        ___        ───
txt                                 Ca-rang     wrek-sa

anl                                     Barang Miring



sar    .       .       .      2      5      3       2        1
```

```
sar    .    6    5    .    .    5    6    1    2N
pes         5    5 .5  6 1̭   5 .3̭ 2.1̭   2    3̭.1̭2
txt         Wrek – sa wi  –   lis tanpa  pa – tra
anl                   Barang Miring


sar    .    3    6    5    .    .    5    .

sar    5    5    .    6    1    6    5    6N
pes                        1̭   2 3̭5 2 .1̭  6̭.56̭
txt                        No- ra     gampang
anl                   Barang Miring


sar    .    .    5    1    5    3    2    1

                                              N
sar    .    6    5    .    5    6    1    2G
pes                        .5 5 .561̭ 5.3̭ 2.1̭ .2 3̭.1̭2
txt                    Wong urip nèng ngalam donya
anl                        Barang Miring
```

Appendix 3: Pathet Sanga

Minggah Ladrang *Éling-éling Kasmaran*

```
sar    3     2     1     6.    5.    6.          1       2N

pes                            .3  5 / .   .6 5 3 2
txt                            Je-neng     sé - la
anl                            S  Sh       M or S Cc


sar    3     2     1     6P.   5.    6.          1       2N

pes                            5  5.3  3 .2   5/.653 2
txt                            Wader kalèn seson-dè- ran
anl                                S 3.1      M or S Cc


sar    3     5     .     .P    5.    6.          1       2N

pes                            .1  2  6   1/ .5 .532
txt                            A- pu          ran-ta
anl                                S 2.2         S Cf


                                                         N
sar    1     6.    1     5P.   1     6.          1       2G

pes                            5  5  1  61 .5/ 5 .653 2
txt                            Yèn wonten lepat ka-wu- la
anl                                S 1.2         S Cd
```

167

sar	3	2	1	6	5	6	1	2N
pes					.5 5 .3	323 .2	5/6.5	3.2
txt					Para-bé Sang	Mara	Bangun	
anl					S 3.1	M or	S Cc	

sar	3	2	1	6P	5	6	1	2N
pes					.5 5.1	656 1.6	5/1.65	3.2
txt					Sepat domba	kali	O - ya	
anl					S 1.2		S Ce	

sar	3	5	.	.P	5	6	1	2N
pes					.1 2.6	1.5	3.2/ .5	6.532
txt					Aja dolan	lan	wong priya	
anl					S 2.2		S Cd	

								N
sar	1	6	1	5P	1	6	1	2G
pes					.5 5.3	323 .2	5/5.65	3 232//
txt					Geng rèmèh	nora	prasa - ja	
anl					S 3.1		S Cd	

Appendix 3: Pathet Sanga

```
sar    .    3    .    2    .    6    .    5

pes    .3 5 / 53 565 3.2//  1 2 .6 1 / .5 3 2.5  5

txt    Sayèng ka - ga,    Kaga kresna mangsa sawa

anl    S Sh    S Cd        S 2.2        S Aa



sar    .    1    .    6    .    3    .    2N

pes              .5 5.5 6Ɩ .Ɩ 656 Ɩ 5.Ʒ 2.Ɩ .23.Ɩ2

txt              Wong susila Laga-ké a-nuju  prana

anl                        Barang Miring



sar    .    3    .    2    .    6    .    5P

pes                   .1 2.6 1/.5 3 2.5   5

txt                   Midering rat angalangut

anl                        S 2.2    S Aa



sar    .    1    .    6    .    3    .    2N

pes              1 2.32 .161.5/5 56165 3.2

txt              Lela- na ja-jah nega- ri

anl                        S 2.3    S Ce
```

169

```
sar    .    3    .    5    .     6      .     5P
                                . . . .    .. .  .
pes                           61.1 161 1.6 5612/2.6 1.65
txt                           Mubeng tepining sa- mo- dra
anl                                   S 3.2        S Ca


sar    .    1̇    .    6    .     3      .     2N
                               .  . ⌐⎺  .⎺  ⎺⎺  ⎺⎺
pes                           1 2.1  6 1. 5 2/2325/.5321
txt                           Sumengka hanggraning wu-kir
anl                                   S 2.1    S P Aa S Cc


sar    .    1̇    .    6    .     1̇      .     5P
                               ⎺⎺ ⎺⎺ ⎺  ⎺⎺
pes                           2 2.1 161 .6 2 /.321 6.5
                                  .      .          . .
txt                           A-nalasak  wana  wa- sa
anl                                   S 3.1      S Ce


sar    .    1̇    .    6    .     3      .     2N
                                  . ⎺⎺  ⎺
pes                           5 5 561̇ 5.3̇ 2.1̇ .2 3̇.23̇1̇2
txt                           Tumurun ing jurang trebis
anl                                  Barang Miring
```

170

Appendix 3: Pathet Sanga

```
                 .                      .                  .N
sar    .     1      .     6       .     2      .      1G

                              . .  —    . .  —      —      —.
pes                           1 2 .6  161 .6  5/  .5  6561

txt                           Tumurun ing jurang tre-bis

anl                                  S 2.2           S Bb*
```

Ngelik

```
                 .                .                  .                  .
sar    .     2      .     1       .     3      .      2

                                       .      .                   . .
pes                                    2      2   .  6 / 6  1.2//

txt                                    Go – nas       ga–nès

anl                                        S Sh     M or S Be
```

```
                 .                                   .                  .
sar    .     1      .     6       .     3      .      5N

                   .      —      —               . .— .      —
pes          5     1 / .5 3 5 .2 6//      1  2.6 1 / .5 3 2.5 5//

txt          Ra   –  mané dhéwé,        Ngudiya mring kang utama

anl            S Sh      S Bc              S 2.2         S Aa
```

---

*This cèngkok is sung only before the ngelik.

sar	.	2	.	1	.	2	.	6P
pes	5 5 .6 1					12.32.161/.5 5.32/2.356 6		
txt	Rama					Sayek- ti ka-lamun su - wung		
anl	S Be					S 2.3 S Cf S Ba		

sar	.	5	.	3	.	1	.	2N
pes						5 5.1 656 1.5/5 5.3 2/.356		
txt						Tangèh miri - ba kang warni		
anl						S 1.2 S P Cf S Be		

sar	.	3	.	5	.	6	.	5P
pes						61.1 1 .16 5612/ 2.6 1.65		
txt						Lan sira pepujan ing-wang		
anl						S 3.2 S Ca		

sar	.	1	.	6	.	3	.	2N
pes						1 2 2165 5.61.5/5 1652/5.321		
txt						Ma- nawa da- saring bu-mi		
anl						S 2.1 S P Ce S Cc		

Appendix 3: Pathet Sanga

sar	.	1	.	6	.	1	.	5P
pes					2 2.1 1 61 .6	2/3.21	6.565
txt					Miwah luhu-ring	haka -	sa
anl					S 3.1		S Ce

								N
sar	.	1	.	6	.	3	.	2G
pes					5 5 561 5 .3	2.1 .2	3.2312
txt					Tuwin jroning	jala-	nidhi
anl					Barang Miring		

Ketawang *Sinom Parijata*, Sléndro Pathet Sanga
(Sindhèn Cèngkok by Gitosaprodjo)

sar	6	6	.	.	2	3	2	1N
pes						5 6165/	.2 1 6 1
txt						Trahing	nata
anl						S 1.1	S Ch

								N
sar	3	2	1	6P	2	1	6	5G
pes		1 2/	.	232 1 6//	2 2 1 1 6	2/.2 6	1.65
txt		Ya mas	ya	mas,	Garwa risang	danan	Jaya
anl		S Sh	S Cd		S 3.1		S Ca

173

```
sar    6       6       .       .       2       3       2      1N
       .       .

pes                                    5    6165 /.2    16   1
                                             .
txt                                   Dèn  pra -  yit-na

anl                                    S 1.1        S Ch


                                                              N
sar    3       2       1      6P       2       1       6     5G
                               .
pes          1 2/    .  232  1 6//    . . .  .
                        ———    —·      1 2 1 61/ .5 3. 25   5
                                          —              —
txt          Radèn   ra - dèn,     Sabarang haywa sembrana

anl          S Sh    S Cd             S 2.1        S Aa
```

Ngelik

```
       .       .
sar    1       1       .       .       2       3       5      6N
                                       .  ... . .
pes                                    1 232 161 .5 2/.2356 6
                                         —   —        ———
txt                                Nula-da la-ku u-ta - ma

anl                                    S 2.3        S Ba


                                       .               .      N
sar    3       5       3      2P       1       6       1     5G

pes                                    . . .   .
                                       1 2 1 61/ .5 3. 25   5
                                           —
txt                                Tumraping wong tanah Jawi

anl                                    S 2.1        S Aa
```

Appendix 3: Pathet Sanga

```
sar    .    6    2·   1·   3      2       1      6N·

pes                          ·  ·   ·
                          1  2  1  6561.5  2/.232  16·

txt                       Wong agung ing Ngèksiganda

anl                              S 2.1        S Cd


                                                         N
sar    .    2    .    1P    .      6·      .      5G·

pes                          2 2 1 6· 2/.26· 1. 65·· /

txt                       Panembahan Sènapa-ti

anl                              S 3.1      S P Ca


sar    2    2    .    .     3      5       3      2N

pes  6 1 2                       3 3 561· .5 5/.565 32/.3
     ·

txt                          Kepati   amar-su- di

anl  S Be                        S 1.1    S P Cd


                                                         N
sar    1    1    6·   5P·   2      3       2      1G

pes  2 1                     ·  ·  · ·
                          1  2  1  61 . 5 2/.25 321

txt                       Sudané ha-wa lan nepsu

anl  M or S Cf                   S 2.1       S Cb
```

```
sar    5      6      2      1      3      2      1      6N
                                                         .
                                          .  ... .
pes                                    6  1 2161.5 2/232 16
                                          ‾‾‾‾       ‾‾  ‾.
txt                                    Pinesu  tapa  bra-ta

anl                                        S 2.1      S Cd


                                                           N
sar    .      2      .      1P     .      6      .      5G
                                          .              .
pes                                    2 2 1 1 6 2/.26 1. 65
                                              .    ‾‾  ‾‾‾‾
txt                                    Tanapi ing siyang ratri

anl                                        S 3.1      S Ca


       .             .             .      .      .      .
sar    1      6      1      5      2      3      2      1N
                                          .      .       .
pes                                    1  2/  .  6 5  6 1//
                                                   ‾‾‾‾‾
txt                                    A- ma      ma  -  ngun

anl                                        S Sh      S Bb


                                                           N
sar    3      2      1      6P     2      3      2      1G
                                   .
pes           5      2      232    16        2  2  .  232  121
                            ‾‾‾    ‾.                 ‾‾‾  ‾‾‾
txt           Kar-yè  -    nak    ing      tyas sa - sa - ma*
```

---

*During the last kenongan of this piece, the pesindhèn sings the gérong part, rather than a separate sindhèn melody. For this reason, I have not labelled patterns in this kenongan.

Appendix 3: Pathet Sanga

Srepegan, Sléndro Pathet Sanga (Sindhèn Cèngkok by Tukinem)

```
                 P                P                P                N
sar   6N    5N       6N    5N    2N    3N    2N    1GS

                 .         .    .         .
pes              1    2    1    6 1    5    2 /    3  2  1  1

txt1             Ri - ris har- da    Ri- ris  har  -  da

txt2             Har- da- ning wong  lu- mak - sa   -  na

an1                        S 2.1             M or S Cf


                 P                P                P                P
sar   2N    1N       2N    1N    3N    2N    3N    2N

pes1                                     1        2 /

txt1                                     Ya       mas

an11                                       S Sh

pes2                                  2  2  2  2  2  2

txt2                                  Dresing karsa Mama-

an12                                       S 3.1


                 P                P                P                P
sar   5N    6N       1N    6N    1N    6N    1N    6N
      .     .              .           .           .
pes1  2   3    2     1        6    6
                               .    .
txt1  ya                      mas

an11              S Cd

pes2  1   1 6 2/  2   3   2   1    6
              .                    .
txt2  yu hayuning Pra  -  ja

an12              S Cd
```

177

```
              P               P               P               N
sar   2N     1N     2N       1N      3N      5N      6N      5GS

                     .       .               .
pes                  1       2 /     6   1   6       5        5

txt1                Ri  -   ris     har         -            da

txt2                Ya      mas     ya                       mas

anl                      S Sh               S Cf
```

```
              P               P               P               N
sar   6N     5N     6N       5N      3N      2N      3N      2GS

                                     .
pes                  5       5   6   1 /     5       3   2    2

txt                 Ra  -   ma              ra          -    ma

anl                      S 1.1              S Cf
```

```
              P               P               P               N
sar   3N     2N     3N       2N      3N      5N      6N      5GS

pes                          2       3 / 2   1   2   3        5

txt                         Go  -   nès

anl                      S Sh                S Ba
```

178

Appendix 3: Pathet Sanga

Suwuk[*]

sar	6N	P 5N	3N	P 2N	3N	N 5G
pes		1	2/ 2 6	1	6	5
txt		Go - nès	go -	nès		
anl		S Sh		S Ca		

Ladrang *Sri Wibawa*, Sléndro Pathet Sanga
(Sindhèn Cèngkok by Gitosaprodjo)

sar	1	6	1	2	1	6	1	5N

sar	1	6	1	2P	1	6	1	5N
pes					1 2 / .	2 6 1.6 5//		
txt					Trahing	na- ta		
anl					S Sh	S Ca		

sar	2	2	.	.P	5	3	2	1N
pes	6 1 2				5 6 5 161 .5	2/.232 1.6		
txt	Ya mas				Garwa risang	Danan Ja-ya		
anl	S Be				S 1.3	S Cd		

---

[*]This suwuk is played after the gatra 2121 3565GS in this recording.

Mode in Javanese Music

```
                                                              N
sar      6      6      2      1P      6      5      3      5G
         .      .                     .      .      .

pes  1   6//                   2222 2 2 11 6 2/.2 6 1.65
         .                                    .     . .
txt                      Dèn prayitna Sabarang haywa sembrana
an1                                   S 3.1            S Ca*


sar      1      6      1      2      1      6      1      5N
                .                           .             .

pes1                                 1  2 / .  2 6 1.6 5//
                                              .    . . .
txt1                                 Jarwa     mu- dha
an1l                                 S Sh      S Ca

pes2                                 222222 1 1 6 2/.2 6 1.65
                                              .      .    . .
txt2                     Jarwa mudha mudhané Sang Prabu Kresna
an12                                 S 3.1            S Ca


sar      1      6      1      2P     1      6      1      5N
                .                           .             .
                                            . . .   .
pes1            5  6 1  2   2//       121  61/ .5 3 . 25 5
                .  .                          -
txt1            Ra-mané dhé-wé,  Mudhané Sang Prabu Kresna
an1l                S Ba             S 2.1       S Aa
                                     . . . . . .  . .
pes2                                 111111 2 61/ .5 3 . 25 5
                                              -          -
txt2                     Pupung anom Ngudi sarananing Praja
an12                                 S 2.2          S Aa
```

---

*This gongan is played only once. The two subsequent gongan are played alternately.

Appendix 3: Pathet Sanga

```
            .
sar    1      6      5      6P      5       3       2       1N
                                    .  .  .  .
pes                                 1 2 1 61 . 5 2/.232 1 6
                                        ‾            ‾     ‾
                                                             .
txt                                 Nalikani- ra ing da-lu

anl                                         S 2.1       S Cd


                                                           N
sar    6      6      2      1P      6       5       3      5G
       .      .
                                    .  .  .  .
pes 1 6//                           1 2 1 61/ .5 3 . 25 5
    ‾                                         ‾        ‾
txt                                 Wong agung mangsah semèdi

anl                                         S 2.1      S Aa


Ngelik

sar    .      .      5      3      2       3       5       6N
                                   .  .  .  .
pes1                               1 2 1 61/ .5 532/2356 6
                                             ‾     ‾
txt1                               Sirep kang bala wa- na - ra

anl1                                      S 2.1    S Cf   S Ba
                                   .  .  .  .
pes2                               1 2 1 61 . 5 2/.2356 6
                                             ‾      ‾
txt2                               Sirep kang bala wa-na- ra

anl2                                      S 2.1        S Ba
```

```
sar    2·      3·      2·     1P·     6       5       3      5N

pes                                 1 2 1 6̇1̇/ .5 3 . 25 5

txt                                 Sadaya wus samya guling

anl                                      S 2.1      S Aa


sar    1·      6       5      6P     5       3       2      1N

pes                                 5 6 5 1̇6̇1 .5 2/.232 1.6

txt                                 Nadyan ari  sudarsa- na

anl                                      S 1.3      S Cd


sar    6·      6·      2      1P     6·      5·      3·     5G·

pes   1 6                           2 2 1 1 6 2/.6 2 16 5
        ·                                 ·       ·  · ·

txt          Wus dangu nggèn ira guling

anl                                      S 3.1      S Cb
```

Ketawang *Suba Kastawa*, Sléndro Pathet Sanga
(Sindhèn Cèngkok by Kenang Darmoredjono)

```
sar    .      1      .      6      .      1      .      5N·

pes   1 2 / . 2 321 6//            1 2 / .6 2 16165//

txt   Ra-ma      ra - ma          Su-ku  palwa

anl   S Sh     S Cd               S Sh      S Cb
```

Appendix 3: Pathet Sanga

```
                                                             N
sar    .     1     .     6P    .     1     .     5G
                                    .                      .

pes    2 3 5 3 2/ 2  321 6//      221161 .6 2/6216165
                    ____  .           ..          . ...

txt    -Man éman éman é -  man,  Palwa kandheg ing samodra

anl        S 4.1      S Cd            S 3.1      S Cb


sar    .     1     .     6     .     1     .     5N
                                    .                      .

pes    1  2 / .  2 321  6//       1  2 / .6 2  16165//
                  ____   .                 .    ____
                                              . ..

txt    Ra-ma      ra -  ma       Su-ku  palwa

anl    S Sh       S Cd            S Sh       S Cb


                                                             N
sar    .     1     .     6P    .     1     .     5G
                                    .                      .

                                          .. .
pes    2 3 5 3 2/ 2  321 6//      1261/ . 5 3  25  5
                    ____  .                        __

txt    -Man éman éman é -  man, Palwa kandheg ing samodra

anl        S 4.1      S Cd            S 2.2      S Aa


Ngelik

              .           .
sar    .     2     .     1     .     6     .     5N

                                          .. .
pes                               1261/ . 5 3  25  5
                                                   __

txt                               Yekti éndah adi lu-hung

anl                                   S 2.2      S Aa
```

183

```
sar    .    2    .    1P    .    6    .    5G
                                      .        N

pes                          2 2 1 161 .6 2/6 16165
                                     .   .  .   . . .
txt                          Nenggih candraning Nagari

anl                                S 3.1      S Cf


sar    .    2    .    1    .    6    .    5N
            .         .                        .

pes                              .. .
                              1261/ . 5 3  25  5
txt                           Indonesi-a mardi- ka

anl                                S 2.2      S Aa


sar    .    2    .    1P    .    6    .    5G
                                      .        N
                                               .
pes                          2 2 1 161 .6 2/6 16165
                                     .   .  .   . . .
txt                          Mardika ma-deg pribadi

anl                                S 3.1        S Cf


sar    .    2    .    1    .    2    .    6N
                                               .
pes 165 6     1                  .. . .
    .. .                      1261 5 2/ . 2321 6
txt Ra- ma                    Andedasar Pancasi- la    .

anl     S Bb                        S 2.2    S Cd
```

184

Appendix 3: Pathet Sanga

```
                                                      N
sar   .    2    .    1P    .    6    .    5G
                              .                .

pes                          221 161 .6 2/6 16165
                                 ‾‾‾  .   .   .  ‾‾‾‾‾
                                          ·   ·    · ··
txt                          Sinembuh luhuring budi

anl                             S 3.1      S Cf
```

185

APPENDIX 4

GENDHING IN SLÉNDRO NEM
WITH SINDHÈN NOTATION

Ayak-ayakan, Sléndro Pathet Nem (Sindhèn Cèngkok by Tukinem)

				N				N
sar								6G

				N				N
sar	.	5N	.	6P	.	5N	.	6P

				.N		.		.N
sar	.	2N	.	1P	.	3N	.	2P

```
                             N
sar    .       6N      .    5GS

                             .
pes                  5   6 / 1  6

txt                  Ri- ris  har-

anl                  M Sh      ?



                             N    .                    N
sar   [:3     2N     3      5P    1      6N     5      6P

                                       .    .  .
pes   5//     2      2   3  5//         1    2  1      6//

txt   da,     Ya    mas                Ya   mas

anl                  ?                         M Cf



                             N                         N
sar    5      3N     5      6P    3      2N     1      2GS

                             .         .
pes                  6       1  6   2   6   3/ 5 3 2 3 2//

txt1                 Har - daning wong lumak-sa  -  na

txt2                 Wong   mardi  pi-kir ra- har  -  ja

anl                              M 1.3              ?



                             N                         N
sar    5      6N     5      3P    5      6N     5      3P

             .    .                      .    .
pes    5   6  1  2  / 6  5  3 3//    5  6  1  2/ 6 5 3 3//

txt    Ra-ma           ra  -  ma,    Dresing    kar - sa

anl       M 1.1        M Cf             M 1.1    M Cf
```

Appendix 4: Pathet Nem

```
                        N                              N
sar   2      1N    2    6P     2      1N     2     3GS
                        .
pes   3 2  1//              6      6 5 5 3 6/ 6 5  3//
txt   Ra - ma              Ma - ma-yu ha-yuning Pra-ja
anl   M or S Cf                    M 3.1        M Cf


                        N                              N
sar   5      6N    5     3P    2      1N     3     2P
pes      5 6 1 2/ 6 5   3// 3     2    1//       2 2 2
txt      Ra-dèn      ra - dèn, Ra   -   ma,    Witing kla-
anl         M 1.1       M Cf        M or S Cf


                       N                               N
sar   6      5N    3    5GS    3      2N     3     5P
      .      .     .    .      .      .      .     .
pes   2 2 2 1 1 6 2/ 2 6 1 6 5//          1  2/ 2 6 1 6
                  .      .   . .                   .      .
txt   pa Kalapa kang masih mudha,        Sa-lu-gu- né
anl        S 3.1        S Ca              S Sh    S Ca


                       N                               N
sar   3      2N    3    5P     2      3N     5     3P
      .      .     .    .
pes   5                            2  2 1 6/ 1 2  3//
      .                                  .
txt                                Ya mas
anl                                  M Cf      M Be
```

189

```
                        N
sar    5       2N      3      5GS:]

                        .
pes    5  6 /  1       6      5

txt    Sa-lu - gu  -   né

anl    M Sh            ?
```

Suwuk[*]

```
                            N                              N
sar    6       6N      5    6P     3       2N      1       6G
                                                           .
pes                3  3 3 3 3 3 2  2  1  3/ 1 3 2 1 6
                                                           .
txt            Sa-luguné wong mardi pikir ra-har  -   ja

anl                            M 3.1              M Cb
```

Gendhing *Kabor*, Kethuk 2 Kerep,
Sléndro Pathet Nem (Sindhèn Cèngkok by Tukinem)

```
sar    2       2       .      .      2       2      .       3


                       .                            .
sar    5       6       1      .      5       6      1       6N
```

---

[*]This suwuk is played after the gatra

```
            N
3    2    1    2GS
```

in this recording. If the piece continues instead of stopping at the suwuk, the
pesindhèn must adjust the text.

Appendix 4: Pathet Nem

```
sar    5      5      .      .      5      6      5      3

                                                        N
sar    5      6      5      3      2      1      6      5G
                                                 .      .

sar    .      5      5      5      2      2      3      5
              .      .      .      .      .      .      .

sar    2      3      5      6      2      1      6      5N
       .      .      .      .                    .      .

sar    3      3      .      .      3      3      5      3
                                                  .   .
pes                                        5   6  1   2/
                                           _____
txt                                        Wi-ting
anl                                           M 1.1


                                                        N
sar    6      5      3      5      3      2      1      2G
                                  .      .
pes    6 5  3//              6  1  6  2  6  3/ 5 3  6532//
       ____                                   ___  ____
txt    kla - pa             Kalapa kang masih mu - dha
anl    M Cf                            M 1.3       M Cb


sar    .      5      .      3      .      5      .      2
pes       3  5 / 6    5     3//           5  6 / 63 6532//
                     ___                        ___ ____
txt       Ra-ma  ra - ma                  Sa-lu- gu-né
anl       S Sh      M Cf                   M Sh    M Cb
```

```
sar    .    5      .      3      .      5      .    2N
                   ..                          .    .
pes          6   612/ 653  3//       6 1 6 2  6 3/ 53  2//
txt          Ra–dèn  ra – dèn,  Wong mardi pikir raharja
anl          M 1.1    M Cf              M 1.3    M or S Cf


sar   5    5      .      .      5    6    5    3
                                          ..
pes        5   3 /   2   3 5//         5 612/ 53  3
txt        Ra     –     ma            Gonès  go– nès
anl        S Sh       ?               M 1.1    ?


                                                    N
sar   5    6      5      3      2    1    6      5G
           . .           ..                 .    .
pes     6  1 2  6  6/ 216 53//  5 6 5 35  2  1 / 6 2165
txt   –Man é–man é–man é – man,  Wong mardi pikir raharja
anl        M 1.1        M Ce          N           S Cb


sar    .    5      5      5      2    2    3    5
            .      .      .      .    .    .    .
pes                                1  2.3 2 3 32 165
txt                              Ri–ris    har–da
anl                              Barang Miring
```

192

Appendix 4: Pathet Nem

```
sar    2      3      5      6     2     1     6      5N
       .      .      .      .                 .

pes               1 / 2 3 2 1  6//   2 2 1 1 6 2/ 6 2 1 6 5
                                             .      . .

txt               Ra- ma              Hardaning wong lumaksana

anl               ?       S Cd              S 3.1      S Cb
```

Ngelik

```
sar    6      6      .      .     6     6     5      6
                                                    . .  ..
pes          3 / 6 5 3 5 6                    2 3/ 12
                                                    __
txt          Ra- ma                           Dresing kar-

anl    M Sh          ?                        M Sh
```

```
       .      .      .      .     .     .     .      N
sar    1      1      2      1     3     2     1      6G

       .                          .  .  .  . .
pes    1 6 6                      2  3  2  1 2/ 6 53
       __                                        __
txt           sa                  Ma-ma-yu ha - yu-ning

anl    M Cf                             M 1.1     M Aa
```

```
sar    .      .      6      2     .     .     2      3

                     . .  . .  .
pes    6 6// 5 6 Ɩ 6 Ɩ 6  Ɩ 6 Ƀ 2  Ƀ Ƀ 2

txt    Praja,  Ya mas        ya      mas

anl              Barang Miring
```

193

```
sar    5      6      1̇      .        5      6      1̇     6N

pes                                   2   2   2̇3̇5̇  3̇2̇ 1̇ 65 6  1̇61̇56
txt                                   Witing kla- pa Witing klapa
anl                                         Barang Miring


sar    5      5      .      .        5      6      5      3

pes           1̇ 6  5  5//                    5 61̇2/ 61653 3//
txt           Ra  -  ma                      Gonès  go - nès
anl              Barang Miring               M 1.1   M Cd


                                                          N
sar    5      6      5      3      2      1      6      5G

pes      6  1̇ 2  6  6/ 21̇6 53//  5  6 5 35  2  1 / 62 165
txt    -Man é-man é-man é - man, Kalapa kang masih mudha
anl          M 1.1      M Ce           N          S Cb
```

Transition Gongan[*]

```
sar    .      5      5      5      2      2      3      5

pes                                1   2 /  2   6
txt                                Sa- lu - gu -
anl                                      S Sh
```

---

[*]The transition gongan leads directly to Ladrang *Krawitan*.

Appendix 4: Pathet Nem

```
sar   2      3      5      6      2      1      6      5N
      .      .      .      .                    .      .

pes      1      6                    5
                   .                 .

txt      né

anl                    S Ca
```

```
sar   6      6      .      .      6      6      5      6

pes      3   5         6

txt      Go- nès

anl         S Be
```

```
        .      .      .      .      .      .      .      N
sar     1      1      2      1      3      2      1      6G

                                    .  .  .  . .
pes                                 2  3  2  1 2/ 6 5 36 6

txt                                 Wong mardi pikir raharja

anl                                      M 1.1      M Aa
```

Ladrang *Krawitan*, Sléndro Pathet Nem (Sindhèn Cèngkok by Gitosaprodjo)

```
sar   .      5      .      3      .      5      .      6N
             .             .             .             .

pes                                 2   3 /  3 1     2.1 6
                                                         .

txt                                 Trahing na  -   ta

anl                                 M Sh      M Ca
```

Mode in Javanese Music

```
sar   .   5   .   3P   .       5      .      6N
                          .  .  ..
pes                       2  3  2  12 /  6  5  3  6   6
                                    ‾‾
txt                       Garwa risang Danan Ja-ya
anl                           M 2.1        M Aa


sar   .   5   .   6P   .       5      .      6N
                             .  .              .
pes                       6  1  2  . 6/ 3 .5 6 1
                                 ‾‾       ‾‾‾‾‾
text                      Dèn pra-yit na
anl                           M 1.1       M Ba


              .           .           .            N
sar   .   2   .   1P   .       2      .      6G
                          ...  ..
pes                       232  12 /  6  5  3  6   6
                               ‾‾
txt                       Sabarang haywa sembrana
anl                           M 2.1        M Aa


sar   .   3   .   5    .       6      .      5N
pes       5  3 2 5 . 5  5//      5  6 / .3 2  5   5
             ‾‾                        ‾‾‾‾
txt       Ra-mané    dhéwé      Jarwa  mu  -  dha
anl           S Aa              M Sh        ?
```

196

Appendix 4: Pathet Nem

```
sar    .    3    .    6P    .    5      .    3N
                                              .
pes         3    2  6  6//        6655  3  6/6165 3//
txt         Ya          mas,  Mudhané Sang Prabu Kresna
anl              ?                   M 3.1      M Cd


sar    .    5    .    2P    .    3      .    2N
pes       2  3 /  1 2    2//      2  3 /  1 2    2//
txt       Ra-dèn ra  -  dèn,      Pupung a  -  nom
anl       M Sh      M Bf          M Sh      M Bf


                                               N
sar    .    6    .    5P    .    3      .     2G
                                   .    ...
pes        5   3 2 5  5 5//    6 1 6 212  6  3/  21 2//
txt        Ra- mané dhéwé,    Ngudi sara-naning Praja
anl             S Aa              M 1.3       M Ch


'
sar    .    3    .    5    .     6      .     3N
                                              .
pes    2    2    3    5//       5 6 / 6 3  5 6 1//
txt    Ya   mas                 Sendhon nén - dra
anl              ?              M Sh      M Ba
```

197

```
sar    .      1̇      .    6P    .      5         .      3N
pes        1  2  1     6  6//      232 12/ 6   653/3561 1//
txt        Ra        —    dèn,    Arané re-si wa- na - ra
anl              M Cf              M 2.1  M P Cf  M Ba


sar    .      1̇      .    6P    .      5         .      3N
pes        1  2  1     6  6//       5  6 /    6 1 6 5   3//
txt        Go        —    nès      Haywa   mun  —   dur
anl                 M Cf            M Sh        M Cd


                                                        N
sar    .      2      .    3P    .      6         .     5G
pes   365    32//                565 35 . 2 1/ 62   1.65
txt   Ra –   dèn               Wong anom labuh naga-ra
anl       M Cb                             N        S Cb


sar    .      3      .    2     .      6         .      5N
pes                             1  2 /    621      6 5
txt                             Je-ruk    gan - da
anl                                     S Sh       S Cb
```

Appendix 4: *Pathet Nem*

```
sar    .      3      .      2P     .       3      .      2N
                                   ·                     ·
pes                                3 3 2 2   1  3/ 12   2//
txt                                Busana geming pandi-ta
anl                                        M 1.3      M Bf


sar    .      3      .      2P     .       3      .      2N
pes           2    1 6/  12 2//        5   6 /  3 2 5   5//
txt           Ra   -    dèn            A- nu - ru  -   ta
anl              M Cf   M Bf           M Sh         ?


                                                          N
sar    .      5      .      3P     .       6      .      5G
                                                          ·
       · ·          ·
pes    6 612/   6165    3//     565 35    21 / 62 1.65
txt    Ya mas   ya      mas,    Obahing jaman sa-mantya
anl    M 1.1    M Cd                      N      S Cb


sar    .      3      .      2      .       6      .      5N
              ·             ·
pes                                5   6 / 6535          5//
txt                                Trahing na  -   ta
anl                                M Sh          ?
```

199

```
sar     .     2̇     .     1̇P    .     2̇     .     6N

pes     1̇  2̇ /  6 5 1̇   1̇//   2̇ 3̇ 2̇ 1̇2̇/  6 5  3̇6  6//

txt     Ya  mas  ya     mas,   Garwa risang Danan Jaya

anl       S Sh       ?              M 2.1       M Aa


sar     .     5     .     6P    .     5     .     6N

pes     1̇  2̇  1̇  6    6//   2̇ 3̇ 2̇ 1̇2̇/ 6 653/ 561̇ 1̇

txt     Ra         –    dèn,   Dèn prayitna Dèn prayitna

anl              M Cf           M 2.1   M P Cf   M Be


sar     .     2̇     .     1̇P    .     2̇     .     N
                                                    6G

pes                          2̇ 3̇ 2̇ 1̇2̇ / 6 5  3̇6  6

txt                          Sabarang haywa sembrana

anl                             M 2.1       M Aa
```

Gendhing *Lokanata*, Kethuk 2 Kerep, Sléndro Pathet Nem
(Sindhèn Cèngkok by Ki Wasitodipuro)

```
sar     .     .     1     2     1     6     5     3
                                      .     .     .
```

Appendix 4: Pathet Nem

```
sar    6    5    3    2    .        3       5        6N
       .    .    .    .            .       .        .
                                    ‾       ‾
pes                              .2   3   .5   3/ 3.1 2.16//
                                                    ‾‾  ‾‾
txt                              Sa-ji         sis-wa

anl                                 ?          M Ca


sar    .    .    1    2    1        6       5        3
                                   .       .        .
                        ‾                   ..       ‾‾‾
pes                   6  .2  2//          .6 6.12 / 6 153  3
                      .
txt                   Ra - ma,           Gonas   ga - nès

anl                        M Bd           M 1.1   M Cd


sar    6    5    3    2    .        3       5        6N
       .    .    .    .            .       .        .
       ‾                            ‾‾      ‾‾
pes                              .3 3 .2 212 .1 3/ 1.3 2.16//
                                       ‾‾‾      ‾‾‾      .
txt                              A-rané ba- sa na-wa- la

anl                                     M 3.1        M Cb


sar    2    2    .    .    2    2    .    3

pes    2    2    2 16/  1.2
                   ‾‾   ‾‾
                   .
txt    Mas mas ya    mas

anl       M Cf    M or S Cf
```

```
sar   5      5      6      .      3      3      5      6N
                                   ‾‾     .  .     .   . . .
pes                               .2   3 .5    3  /3.1 2.1 6
txt                               Na-dyan        la- mong
anl                                   ?           M Cb


sar   .      .      6      1́     6      5      3      5


                                                          N
sar   2      3      5      6      3      5      3      2G
                                  ‾  ‾‾    .  .‾‾
pes                              .6 1.6 2.12.6 3/3.6 .6532//
txt                              Nyalemong tanpa uka - ra
anl                                      M 1.3        M Cb


sar   5      5      .      .      5      5      2      3

pes   5 3/.2 35
txt   Gen - dhuk
anl   S Sh  ?


sar   5      6      5      3      2      1      2      6N
                                                          .
pes                               .2   3 .5    3  /3.1 2.16
txt                               Ru-bèng        gar-wa
anl                                   ?           M Cb
```

Appendix 4: Pathet Nem

```
sar    3       3       .       .       6       5       3       5

pes    .1  2.1  6/12 3

txt    Ra-ma

anl      M Cf    M Be


sar    2       3       5       3       2       1       2       6N
                                                              ·
pes                                    .5 6.1 6 .53 5.2/3 1.3  2.16//

txt                                    Dustha  wéri Ja-lada - ra

anl                                            N            M Cb


sar    2       2       .       .       2       2       .       3

pes    2   2   2  16/ 1.2

txt    Mas mas ya    mas

anl      M Cf      M or S Cf


sar    5       6       5       3       2       1       6       5N
                                                       ·       ·
pes                                    .1 2 . 3  2/2.6  2165/

txt                                    Kaya      nga- pa

anl                                    S 2.3     S Cb
```

203

Mode in Javanese Music

sar	1	1	.	.	3	2	1	6.
pes	.1̄	1	1̣ 6̣ 5/	6̣.1				
txt	Yadhuk	ya	-	dhuk				
anl		?		S Bf				

sar	.	5̣	3̣	2̣	.	3̣	5̣	N 6G̣
pes					.3	3.2	212	13.53/3.1 3.216̣
txt					Kang	gawé	lara wi-	ya- ga
anl						M 3.1		M Cb

Gendhing *Majemuk*, Kethuk 2, Minggah Kethuk 4,
Sléndro Pathet Nem (Sindhèn Cèngkok by Gitosaprodjo)

sar	.	.	3	.	2	1	2	.
sar	3	2	1	2	6̣	1	3	2N
sar	3	1	2	3	2	1	2	6̣

204

Appendix 4: Pathet Nem

```
sar    .        .        6        1        2        3        5        3N

pes                                        6   Ƅ Ƅ Ƅ   2        3

txt                                        Trahing    na  -  ta

anl                                          Barang Miring


sar    .        .        3        .        3        3        .        5

pes                                        6   1̇ 2̇ .6 3/  5 . 6 1̇

txt                                        Ya mas  ya   mas

anl                                          M 1.1      M Be


sar    6        1̇        5        6        .        5        3        2N

pes    1̇  2̇3/  . 1̇2̇1̇   6//      6 1̇ 6 2̇1̇2 6 3/212  2

txt    Ra-dèn      ra  -  dèn,  Garwa risang Danan Ja-ya

anl    M Sh       M Cf              M 1.3       M Ch


sar    5        6        5        3        2        1        2        6

pes    6 1̇ 2/  6165    3//         2  3/  3 1    2 .1 6

txt    Ya mas   ya      mas,      Ra-dèn ra  -  dèn

anl    M 1.1    M Cd              M Sh      M Ca
```

205

```
sar    .      1      2      3      2      1      2      6N
                                                        .
pes    6  1  2          3  3//      2  3/  1 3    2 .1 6
       .                                  ___         .
txt    Ra- ma-né        dhéwé,      Dèn pra - yit - na

anl        M Ba                     M Sh      M Cb


sar    .      .      3      .      2      1      2      .

pes                  3      3      2 1 2      2
                                   ___ ___
txt                  É  -  ra  -  ma- né

anl                         Gawan


                                                         N
sar    3      2      1      2      6      1      3      2G
                                   .
pes    3      2   1  6  1 2 2//   6 1 6 212 6 3/ 1 2 2
                   .   __          .   ...
txt    É  -  ra- ma-né dhé-wé,    Sabarang haywa sembrana

anl           Gawan                     M 1.3    M Bf


sar    .      .      3      .      2      1      2      .

pes                  3      3      2 1 2      2
                                   ___ ___
txt                  É  -  ra  -  ma- né

anl                         Gawan
```

Appendix 4: Pathet Nem

```
sar   3      2      1      2      6      1      3      2N
                                  .
pes   3      2   1  6   1 2 2//          2 3 / 1 2      2//
txt   É  -  ra- ma-né dhé-wé,           Trahing na  -   ta
anl         Gawan                        M Sh      M Bf


sar   3      1      2      3      2      1      2      6
                                                      .
pes      1   2      3//                  2  3 / 3 1   2.16
txt      Ra- ma                         Trahing na - ta
anl         M Be                         M Sh     M Ca


sar   .      .      6      1      2      3      5      3N
                    .                    .
pes                              6 6 ì 6 ǥ  3 ǥ   2 3
txt                              Garwa risang Danan Jaya
anl                                   Barang Miring


sar   .      .      3      .      3      3      .      5
                                         ..
pes                                    6 12  .  6 3/   5.61
txt                                    Ya mas  ya    mas
anl                                          M 1.1    M Be
```

```
                  .                        .
sar    6          1        5        6      .         5        3        2N

                  .    ..   ...
pes               1   23/  . 121  .  6//           5    6 / . 35      3  2//
                     ‾‾‾        ‾‾‾
txt               Ra-dèn       ra  -  dèn,         Dèn  pra - yit - na

anl               M Sh         M Cf                M Sh        M Cf



sar    5          6        5        3      2       1        2        6
                                                                     .
                      .   .
pes               6  1  2/      6  5  3//          2    3/    3 1 2.1 6
                  ‾‾‾‾‾         ‾‾‾‾‾                         ‾‾  ‾‾‾  .
txt               Ya           mas                 Ra-dèn    ra- dèn

anl               M 1.1        M Cf                M Sh       M Ca



sar    .          1        2        3      2       1        2        6N
                                                                     .
pes    6    1    2    .    .    3   3//             2    3/   3 1 2.1 6
       .                                                     ‾‾  ‾‾‾  .
txt    Ra- ma-né           dhéwé,                  Dèn  pra - yit-na

anl              M Ba                              M Sh       M Ca



sar    .          .        3        .      2       1        2        .

pes                        3        3      2 1 2            2
                                           ‾‾ ‾‾‾
txt                        É    -   ra  -  ma- né

anl                                        Gawan
```

Appendix 4: Pathet Nem

```
                                                                    N
sar    3       2       1       2       6       1       3       2G

pes    3       2   1   6   1 2 2//      6 1 6 212 6  3/ 12   2
                       .                    .   ...
                           ___                          __

txt    É   -   ra- ma-né dhé-wé,   Sabarang haywa sem-bra-na

anl            Gawan                         M 1.3      M Bf


sar    .       .       3       .       2       1       2       .

pes                    3       3       2 1 2       2
                                       ___   _____

txt                    É   -   ra   -  ma- né

anl                            Gawan


sar    3       2       1       2       6       1       3       2N
                                       .
pes    3       2   1   6   1 2 2//          2 3 /   3212    2//
                       .   __                      ____
txt    É   -   ra- ma-né dhé-wé,            Jarwa  mu  -   dha

anl            Gawan                        M Sh   M Ch


sar    3       1       2       3       2       1       2       6
                                                               .
pes    1   2       3//                      2 3 /   31  2.1 6
           _____                              __      .
txt    Ra- dèn                           Jar-wa  mu- dha

anl        M Be                          M Sh   M Ca
```

209

```
sar   .      .      6̣      1       2       3       5       3N

pes          6   6  1̇  6   5       3   5̶     2       3

txt          Mudha - né Sang  Pra- bu            Kres - na

anl                        Barang Miring
```

```
sar   .      .      3       .       3       3       .       5

pes          6̄   1̇̇  2̇       6   3 /         5    6   1̇

txt          Go- nès            go      -       nès

anl                        M 1.1            M Be
```

```
sar   6      1̇      5       6       .       5       3       2N

pes                          2   3/    3212    2

txt                          Pu-pung  a   -    nom

anl                          M Sh     M Ch
```

```
sar   5      6      5       3       2       1       2       6̣

pes       5   6 /   6165    3//         2   3/   3 1    2.16//

txt       Ya mas    ya      mas         Ra-dèn  ra -    dèn

anl       M Sh      M Cd                M Sh    M Ca
```

Appendix 4: Pathet Nem

```
sar    .    1    2    3    2    1    2    6Ṇ

pes        6 1  2 . 3  3//      2  3/  3 1   2.1 6//
txt          Rama-né dhéwé        Pupung  a  -  nom
anl             M Ba            M Sh      M Ca


sar    .    2    .    1    .    2    .    1

pes    1 2  2 3   1//      1 2   2 3   1
txt    Ra-ma ra  -  ma      Ra-dèn ra  - dèn
anl         Gawan              Gawan


                                          N
sar    .    3    .    2    .    1    .    6G

pes                   3333 3 3 2 2  1 3/ 31 2.16
txt                Pupung anom Ngudi sarananing Praja
anl                             M 3.1      M Ca


Minggah

sar    .    .    .    2    .    .    .    1

pes                        2  3 / . 353   21
txt                        Tra-hing na -  ta
anl                        M Sh      M Cd
```

211

Mode in Javanese Music

```
sar    .      .      .      2      .      .      .      1
                                          .    ...
pes                                6  1  6  212  6  3/353  21//
txt                                Garwa risang Danan Jaya
anl                                    M 1.3        M Cd


sar    .      .      .      3      .      .      .      2
pes       1    2      3//              2    3 /   12     2//
txt       Ra- dèn                      Dèn pra - yit  -  na
anl            M Be                        M Sh      M Bf


sar    .      .      .      1      .      .      .      6N
                                                        .
pes       2   3 /   353    21//        3322   1  3/ 31  2.16//
txt           Ra-ma    ra  -  ma,      Sabarang haywa sembrana
anl           M Sh     M Cd                M 3.1       M Ca


sar    .      .      .      1      .      .      .      6
                                                        .
pes    3  6   .  3   6   2  1//     3  1  .  3  1  2  6//
txt    Sa-yuk   sa- yuk se-dya,     Se- dya  se-dya ru-kun
anl            Gawan                        Gawan
```

212

Appendix 4: Pathet Nem

```
sar   .     .       .     1     .     .       .     6
                                                     .
pes   3  6  .  3  6  2  1//    3  1  .  3  1  2  6//
                                                   .
txt   Sa-yuk    sa- yuk se-dya,   Se- dya   se-dya ru-kun

anl           Gawan                      Gawan


sar   .     .       .     1     .     .       .     6
                                                     .
pes    2 2 3 3 3 3 322 3 2 1//   1 2 2 2 2 2 311 2 1 6//
                                                       .
txt   Rujak nanas pantes          Tiwas tiwas nglabuhi
      dèn wadahi gelas,            wong ora welas

anl            Rujak                      Rujak


sar   .     .       .     5     .     .       .     3N
                                            . .    .
pes       5   6/ 56  53 5//       6  1 2/  6165   3//
                 __  __                    ____
txt       Ra- ma-né dhéwé,        Jarwa   mu  -  dha

anl       M Sh      ?             M 1.1     M Cd


sar   .     .       .     5     .     .       .     3
                                                    .
pes       5   6 / 5  3   5//      5  6 /  6165   3//
                                          ____
txt       Ra- ma- né dhé-wé       Jarwa   mu  -  dha

anl       M Sh       ?            M Sh     M Cd
```

213

```
sar    .      .      .      5      .      .      .      6
                                         ...  ..
pes        6 5 6 5 6 5 3 5//        232 12/ . 6 5 . 36 6//
                                          ‾
txt        Gonas ganès wicarané,   Mudhané Sang Prabu Kresna

anl                 ?                   M 2.1      M Aa


                                 .                           .
sar    .      .      .      2      .      .      .      1
           .      .                . . . .            . .
pes      6  1      2//            2 3 1 2   6  3 /561 1//

txt      Ya mas                   Pupung anom Pupung a-nom

anl         M or S Be                   M 2.2      M Be


sar    .      .      .      3      .      .      .      2N
          . . .                       .  ...
pes     6 1 2 3  6  3/ 1 2 3//      616 212   6 3/ 212 2//
                                              ‾
txt     Pupung anom Pupung anom,   Ngudi sarananing Praja

anl              ?       M Be             M 1.3      M Ch


sar    .      .      .      5      .      .      .      3
                                        .  ..            .
pes      5  6 / 5  3   5// 666666 1 12   6  6/6165 3//
                                   ‾               ‾
txt      Ra-ma- né dhéwé, Sendhon nèndra Arané resi wanara

anl         M Sh       ?             M 1.1      M Cd
```

214

Appendix 4: Pathet Nem

```
sar    .     .     .     1     .     .     .     6
                                                 .
pes    1  2    2 3     1// 3333 33 2 2    1  3/.31 2.16
                __                        __        .
txt    Ra- ma  ra - ma, Haywa mundur Wong anom labuh nagara
anl              ?                M 3.1            M Ca


sar    .     .     .     5     .     .     .     3
                                    .     ...
pes                            6 1 6 212 6 6/6165 3
                                     ___
txt                            Nalikani-ra ing da-lu
anl                                 M 1.3      M Cd


sar    .     .     .     1     .     .     .     6N
                                                 .
pes                            3 3 2 2   1 3/ 31 2.16
                                             __    .
txt                            Wong agung mangsah semèdi
anl                                        M 3.1     M Ca


sar    .     .     .     2     .     .     .     1
                         .                       .
pes                            2 3 2 12 6/ 653/3561 1
                               . . . ..        . .
                                   __      ___
txt                            Sirep kang bala wana- ra
anl                                 M 2.1  M Cf  M Ba
```

215

```
sar    .     .     .     2      .     .     .      1
                                     .   ...
pes                            6 1 6 212   6 3/353 21
                                       ‾‾
txt                            Sadaya wus samya guling

anl                                M 1.3      M Cd


sar    .     .     .     3      .     .     .      2
                                   .   ...
pes                            616 212   6 3/ 212 2
                                   ‾‾          ‾‾
txt                            Nadyan ari sudar-sa- na

anl                                M 1.3      M Ch

                                                   N
sar    .     .     .     1      .     .     .      6G
                                                   .
pes                            3 3 2 2   1 3/ 13 2.16
                                         ‾‾     ‾‾‾
txt                            Wus dangu nggènira guling

anl                                M 3.1      M Cb
```

Ladrang *Remeng*, Sléndro Pathet Nem
(Sindhèn Cèngkok by Ki Wasitodipuro)

```
          .
sar    .  6   6    .    6    6    5    6N

       .
sar    1  6   5    3P   2    2    3    2N
```

216

Appendix 4: Pathet Nem

```
sar  [:.       .       6      1P     2      2      3      2N
                                            —             ==
pes                                  .2 3 /  . 5 3232 2//
txt                                  A-mi -  wi -  ti*
anl                                  M Sh           ?


                                                          N
sar  3       2       1       6P     5      6      1      2G
        —       ==      ==       .       .—    . ..—   ==     ==
pes  2 3  5/ 212  3.2  1 6//    6 1.6  2.12.6 3/ 353  6.532
txt  Ya ra-ma ra   -    ma,     Sindhèn sendhoning pradangga
anl  S Sh        S Cd              M 1.3         M Cb


sar  .       2       1       6      5      6      1      2N
                                            —             ==     ==
pes                                  .5 6 /  . 6 5.3  6.532//
txt                                  Tawas   pi -  ta
anl                                  M Sh       M Cb


sar  3       2       1       6P     3      3      5      3N
        ==      ==                      ==
pes  5 .3/ 3.2  1 6                  6 6 6/2 6.3 3.2 .3 5.23
txt  Go  -   nès                     Darpa driya Wisnu garwa
anl  S Sh  M or S Cc                    Barang Miring
```

*This poetic line and the one in the next kenongan comprise the second half of a wangsalan. The first half appears in the last two kenongan on p. 220.

217

sar	.	3	5	6P	i̇	6	5	3N
pes		.3	2 .6	6//		.5 656/.	6.53	3
txt		Ya	ra – ma			Murwèng	gi – ta	
anl		?				M Sh	M Cf	

sar	5	6	i̇	6P	5	3	2	N 3G
pes					.6 6.2	12.66/656	16	.65.3//
txt					Karsa dalem	Sri Narèn	–	dra
anl					M 1.2		M Cd	

sar	6	5	2	1	6.	1	2	3N
pes	35	6.5	3/.653 2	1//	.5	6 1	2/2.16	5.3
txt	Ya rama	rama ra–	ma		Mardi	ba – sa		
anl	M 4.1		M Ce		M 1.1	M Ce		

sar	5	6	i̇	6P	5	3	2	1N
pes					.6 1 2.6	3.2.216	12 3/.3	5.321
txt					Wengku salu	welut		wisa
anl					M 1.1		M Cd	

```
sar     .       1       1       1P      2       3       2       1N
                                                ‾    ‾‾ ‾‾
pes                                     .2  3 /  .3 23 5.3 2.1
txt                                     Karya   wu  -   lang
anl                                     M Sh        M Cd


                                                                N
sar     3       5       3       2P      .       1       6       5G
                                            ‾  ‾‾    ‾‾
pes                                     .5 6.5 3 5.2  6/ 616 2.165//
txt                                     Wewatoné wong Ngawu-la
anl                                             N          S Cb


sar     .       6       1       2       .       1       6       5N
             ‾  ‾‾ ‾‾                        ‾            ‾‾
pes     6   .1/ 13 .1  2//        .1  2 / .  2161 6 2.165
txt     Kanca- né dhéwé            Tambah   ca  -  cah
anl     S Sh       ?               S Sh       S Cb


sar     .       6       1       2P      .       1       6       5N
                                            ‾  ‾‾ ‾‾ ‾       ‾‾
pes                                     .2 2.1 161 .6 2/6.2 1.65//
txt                                     Sembilang taji sepa- sang
anl                                             S 3.1    S Cb
```

219

```
sar    .      6      1      2P    .       1       6      5N
              .                                   .      .
             ___    ___   ___   ___        __    __     __
pes        1 2   6 .1  1 3 .1  2//     .1  2.3  5 2/2.6  .21.65//
                   .                             .       ..
txt          É    ra-ma-né   dhéwé         Mangka      pé - ling
anl                   ?                       ?        S  Cb


       .      .                    .       .       .       N
sar    1      1      .      .P     3       2       1      6G
       __    __    .                __  ... __    __
pes  .5 5   .6   1//               .2 212 .3 12/.6 5 3.6 6
           ___
txt  Rama                         Marang wadya kang leléwa
anl   S  Be                            M 2.2       M Aa


sar    .      6      6      .      6       6       5      6N
                                    __  ... __    __   . .
pes                                .2 2 2ʒʒ 2.ʒ 6ʒ .6 ʒ6ʒʒ6
                                           __
txt                               Basa purwa Basa purwa
anl                                    Barang Miring


       .
sar    1      6      5      3P     2       2       3      2N:]
                                   __  __  __  __  __   __
pes                                .6 6.6 6.ʒ 2ʒʒ2ʒ 6.2ʒ6ʒ ʒ.212
                                                  __         __
txt                               Lalu diwasaning  sur - ya
anl                                    Barang Miring
```

APPENDIX 5

TESTING THE HYPOTHESIS

Ketawang *Sekar Téja* (Sindhèn Cèngkok by Ngabéhi Mardusari)

```
sar    2     2     .     .     2     3     2     1N
                                    . .
pes                              6 1 2 6 3/ 3 535321
                                              ‾‾‾‾‾‾
txt                              Ya mas Sekar pisang
anl                                M 1.1      M Cd


                                                  N
sar    .     3     .     2P    .     1     .      6G
                                                  .
pes                              3 3 3 3 353 3/ 1 216/
                                         ‾‾‾       ‾‾
txt                              Pisang sesaji ning karya
anl                                    M Sh      M P Cf
```

221

```
sar      2      2      .      .      2      3      2      1N

                                    ..
pes     12                   6 12 6 3 2 216123/3 5321
         ‾                             ‾         ‾
txt                              Patut lamun Patut la-mun

anl                                  M 1.1      M Cd


                .             .                  .       N
sar      .      3      .      2P     .      1      .     6G

                                    . . . ..
pes                                 2 3 2 12/ 6  5  3 6  6
                                         ‾             ‾
txt                                 Linulu dan mring sasa - ma

anl                                  M 2.1      M Aa
```

Ngelik

```
                                    .      .      .      .
sar      .      .      6      .      2      3      2      1N

                                    . . . ..              .
pes                                 2 3 2 12/ 6 653/ 356  1
                                         ‾      ‾‾
txt                                 Nalikani-ra ing da- lu

anl                                  M 2.1  M Cf   M Ba


         .      .                                        .N
sar      3      2      6      5P     3      5      6      1G

                                    . . . ..              .
pes                                 2 3 2 12/ 6 65653/ 356 1
                                         ‾      ‾‾‾‾
txt                            Wong Agung mangsah se- mè- di

anl                                  M 2.1      M Cf   M Ba
```

Appendix 5: Testing the Hypothesis

```
                        .       .       .       .       .
sar     .       .       1       2       3       2       1       6N

                                            . . . . . . . .
pes1                                        1 2 2 2/3 1 2  1 6 6
                                                      ____

txt1                                        Sirep kang bala wanara

anl1                                            ?           M Ca

                                          . . . ..
pes2                                       2 3 2 12/  6  5 3 6  6
                                               __         __

txt2                                       Sirep kang bala wana - ra

anl2                                          M 2.1       M Aa



                                                            N
sar     3       5       3       2P      .       1       2    6G
                                                            .

pes                                         3 3 3 3 353/ 3 1 216/
                                                    ___       __.

txt                                         Sadaya wus sam-ya guling

anl                                             M Sh      M P Ca



                                    . .
sar     2       2       .       .       2       3       2       1N

pes     12//                                6 12 6 3/ 6  5 3 5321
        __                                    __          ____

txt                                         Nadyan ari sudarsana

anl M or S Bf                                  M 1.1       M Ce
```

223

```
                                                             N
sar      .      3      .     2P     .      1      .        6G

pes1                                3 3 3 3 353 3/1 3216/12
                                            ‾‾‾      ‾‾‾‾‾‾‾
txt1                                Wus dangu denira guling

anl1                                     M Sh    M P Cb  M or S
                                                           Bf

pes2                                3 3 3 3 353 3/ 1 3 21 6
                                            ‾‾‾      ‾‾‾‾‾
txt2                                Wus dangu denira guling

anl2                                     M Sh       M Cb*
```

Gendhing *K*ocak, Kethuk 4 Kerep,
Minggah Ladrang *Dirada Meta*
(Sindhèn Cèngkok by Soepadmi Soetomo)

```
sar      .      .      2      3      6      5      3      2
                       .      .      .      .      .      .


sar      .      .      2      5      2      3      5      6
                       .      .      .      .      .      .

pes                                              2 3 / 3  1
                                                     ‾‾‾
txt                                              Wiku di -

anl                                              M Sh   M Cb
```

---

*The second cèngkok is sung when the piece ends.

Appendix 5: Testing the Hypothesis

```
sar    .      .      6      1      2      3      5      3

pes   3 2 1 6                 6 6 6161̷2̷ 2̷1̷6 5̷ 32 3 5̷35̷23
      ‾‾‾‾‾‾                        ‾‾‾‾‾ ‾‾‾‾‾     ‾‾‾‾‾
txt   dya                   Aran wi-  wi-ta-né basa

anl                              Barang Miring


sar   5      6      5      3      2      1      6      5N
                                                .      .
pes      6  6 1 2/ 6  5  3  3//      5 616 5 3 5  2 21/
            ‾‾‾‾‾  ‾‾‾‾‾‾‾            ‾‾‾
txt      Ya mas   ya      mas,      A-ran wiwi- ta-né

anl      M 1.1      M Cf                   N


sar    .      5      5      5      2      2      3      5
              .      .      .      .      .      .      .
pes1  6 2 21 6  5                         1   2 3 2/2 6
      ‾‾‾‾‾‾ ‾‾‾                              ‾‾‾‾‾
txt1  ba- sa                             Ya   mas   ya

anl1                                         S  Sh

pes2                                      1   2 3 2/2 6
                                              ‾‾‾‾‾
txt2                                     Go-nès   go-

anl2                                         S  Sh
```

```
sar     .        .       5       6      1      2       3       2

pes1    1   6   5                       5 5 561 1 6 5 6 5 3 21
txt1    mas                             Aran wi-wi   -   tané
anl1       S Ca                              Barang Miring

pes2    2 1 6   5
txt2    nès
anl2       S Cb


sar     .       3       5       2      .      3       5       2

pes     2 3 2 3 1 2//   5  6    2//            3     5   6   2
txt     basa           Go  -  nès              Go      -     nès
anl                    Gawan                      Gawan


sar     5       6       5       3      2      1      6      5N

pes1        6   6 1 2/  6  5 3  3//            5 616 5 3 5  2 21/
txt1        Ya mas      ya     mas,           A-ran wiwi- ta-né
anl1        M 1.1       M Cf                        N

pes2                                          5 616 5 3 5  2 26/
txt2                                          A-ran wiwi- ta-né
anl2                                                N
```

Appendix 5: Testing the Hypothesis

```
sar    .        5      5      5      2      2      3      5

pes1   6 2 1 6 5                1   2   3  2/  2 6 2 1
txt1   ba- sa                  Sru ka  -      ga- gas
anl1     S Cb                      S Sh      S Cb

pes2   1 6 5   5                1   2 3 2 3 2/ 2 6 2 1 6 5
txt2   ba      sa              Sru ka-       ga- gas
anl2     S Cf                      S Sh         S Cb


sar    .        .      5      6      1      2      3      2

pes    6        5                   5 56561 165 3 21 2 32312
txt                                 Mas ya mas Sru kagagas
anl                                    Barang Miring


sar    .        3      5      2      .      3      5      2

pes             3      5   6  6 2//         3      5   6  2//
txt             Go     -      nès          Go     -      nès
anl                 Gawan                       Gawan
```

```
sar    5       6       5       3       2       1       6       5N
                                               .       .
                           .  .
pes1         6   6 1 2/ 6 5 3  3//          5 616 5 3 5   2 21/
                     ___        ___                ___       __
txt1        Ya mas    ya      mas,        Ya mas ya mas Sruka-

anl1        M 1.1     M Cf                          N

pes2                                      1  2/ 2  6  2  2
                                                  _____
txt2                                      Sru ka-ga  -  gas

anl2                                      S  Sh     S Cb


sar    2       3       5       6       3       5       3       2
       .       .       .       .       .       .       .       .
pes1   6 2 1 6 5                           5 6 1 6 1 6/ 6  3
       .     . . .                         . _____
txt1   ga- gas                             Rama         ra-

anl        S Cb                              M Sh     M Cb?

pes2   1 6 5
       _____
       . .


sar    .       .       2       5       2       3       5       6
                       .       .       .       .       .
pes    6 5 3 2                             2  3 / 3    1
       . . . .                                _____
txt    ma                                  Sru ka- ga  -

anl                                        M Sh     M Ca


sar    .       .       6       3       6       5       3       2
                       .       .       .       .       .       .
pes    3 2 1 6                             5 6 1 2 6/63 65
       _____                         . . . . __ __
       .       .                                   .. ..
txt    gas                                 Ya mas   ya mas

anl                                        M 1.1   M Cb?
```

```
                                                           N
sar    .      .      2      3      6      5      3      2G
              ·      ·             ·      ·      ·      ·

pes    3  2
       ·  ·
```

Minggah Ladrang *Dirada Meta*

```
sar    6      3      6      5      6      3      6      2N
       ·      ·      ·      ·      ·      ·      ·      ·


sar    6      3      6      5P     6      3      6      2N
       ·      ·      ·      ·      ·      ·      ·      ·


sar    6      3      6      5P     2      3      5      .N
       ·      ·      ·
                                                      ·
pes                                5      6 /    1 6  5  5//
                                                 ___
txt                               Ka -  wi    dé  -  wa

anl                                M Sh            ?
```

```
                                                           N
sar    2      3      5      3P     2      1      2      6G
                                                       ·
            · ·    · ·
pes1      6   1  2/ 216    653//    3 3 2 2 2 1 3/ 313 3216/
                   ___                            ___ ___·
tx1      -Man  éman é  -   man,   Giwanging wulan purna- ma

anl1      M 1.1     M Ce                 M 3.1        M P Cb

pes2                              3 3 2 2 21 216123/ 31 3216/
                                            __·      __  __·
txt2                              Giwanging wulan pur- na-ma

anl2                                         M 3.2       M P Cb
```

229

```
sar    3       3      6.    5.    2      1       2        6N.

pes1   1  2  3                     2 3 5 3/ 3 1 3 2 1 6/
txt1                               Anjen - tha-ra
anl1     M Be                        ?        M P Cb
pes2   1  2  3                     2 3 5 3/ 3 1  2  1 6//
txt2                               Anjen - tha- ra
anl2     M Be                        ?        M Cb


sar    3       3      6.    5P.   2      1       2        6N.

pes1   1  2  3                     2  3 / 3 1 3 2  1  6
txt1                               An-jen-tha-ra
anl1     M Be                      M Sh      M Cb
pes2   1 216/123                   2  3 / 3 1 3  32 1 6
txt2   Rama                        An-jen-tha -  ra
anl2   M Cf  M Be                  M Sh       M Cb


sar    3       3      6.    5P.   2      1       2        6N.

pes1                               2  3 / 1 3 3216
txt1                               Ya mas ya  mas
anl1                               M Sh      M Cb
pes2                               2  3 / 5 3 216
txt2                               Go-nès go- nès
anl2                               M Sh      ?
```

Appendix 5: Testing the Hypothesis

```
                                                          N
sar    3       3       6     5P    2       1       2     6G
               .             .                           .

pes1                         . . . . .
                             2  3  2 1  2      6  3/ 3 6 6 5
                                   ___
txt1                         Limpat pasang   ing grahi- ta

anl2                                 M 2.1            M Cb

pes2                         . . . . .
                             2  3  2 1  2 / 6 5 3 6 6/ 532//
                                   ___      ___
txt2                         Limpat pasang ing grahita

anl2                                 M 2.1      M P Aa   ?
```

```
               ___  ___  ___  ___
                      .         .
sar    .       .      2    3 5 6 1 . 6 1  5  6N

pes    3 2                  . . . . . . . . .     . .
       ___                  2 2 3 3 3 3 2 1 65 6 16156//
                                                __   __
txt                         Ujung jari Balung ron doning kalapa

anl                                 Barang Miring
```

```
               ___  ___   ___  ___
                      .          .
sar    1       2      .    3P 5 6 1 . 6 1  5  6N

pes    .                    . . . . . . . .     . .
       1 6 5 3232//         2 2 5 3 2 3 2 1 65 6 16156//
       _____                              __  __   __
txt    Ra - ma              Balung ron do-ning kalapa

anl    Barang Miring              Barang Miring
```

231

```
sar    1     2      .     3P 5   6   1  . 6   5   6   1N
pes    1 6 5 3 5 3 2//                   6  612/ 6 6 5 3 5 6
txt    Go  -  nès                     Ka-weng-kuwa
anl    Barang Miring                   M 1.1      M Ba


sar    6   5   6      1      2P      1      6      5      6G(N)
pes    1//      6     6    1 2//     2   3   2  12/ 6   5  36 6
txt               Ya  mas            Sayekti da- di u-sa-da
anl                   M Be               M 2.1      M Aa


sar    .  5  1  6  .  5  1  6  .  5  1  6   5  1  6N
pes                         2 2 5 3232 1 65 6 1615 6
txt                         Witing klapa Witing klapa
anl                              Barang Miring
```

Appendix 5: Testing the Hypothesis


```
sar    1      6      5      3P     2      2      3      2N

pes1       6  1 2/  6  5   3//    6  1  6  2  6  3/ 3212

txt1       Go-nès   go - nès,    Kalapa kang masih mu -

an11       M 1.1    M Cf                M 1.3      M Ch

pes2                               6  1  6  2  6  3/ 36 6532

txt2                               Kalapa kang masih mu-dha

an12                                   M 1.3        M Cb



sar    6      3      6      5P     6      3      6      2N

pes    2//         1 2/ 62 2165//         6126/ 63 6532 2

txt    dha         Gonès gonès             Sa - lu-gu - né

anl                S Sh  S Cb              M 1.1  M Cb?



                                                        N
sar    6      3      6      5P     6      3      6      2G

pes                1 2/ 62 2165//      6 1 6 2 6 3/ 5 3 2 2

txt          Ya mas  ya mas,    Wong mardi pikir rahar- ja

anl                S Sh  S Cb              M 1.3      M Cf
```


233

NOTES

Chapter 1. INTRODUCTION

1. To make matters worse, the saron melody has in the last twenty years been termed *balungan*, which literally means *framework*. Since I do not believe that the saron melody usually functions as the central framework in gamelan music, I have avoided this term.

Chapter 2. SINDHÈNAN IN THE GAMELAN

1. The pesindhèn sometimes sings a cèngkok, called plèsèdan, whose last pitch level is not the same as the last pitch level of a gatra (pp. 49–57).
2. The poetic genres sung by gérong and pesindhèn include: *sekar ageng, sekar tengahan, sekar macapat, sekar dolanan,* and *sekar gendhing.* Some of these are divided into several different types (Gitosaprodjo 1972a:1–2) and Wallis (1973).

Chapter 3. THE RELATIONSHIP OF THE THREE SLÉNDRO PATHET

1. "(<u>Penting</u>: Wiled slendro 9 = wiled slendro manjura turun satu nada.)"
2. "Laras slendro patet enem...Dalam praktek wiled2 (melodi) = tjampuran wiled2 Sl.9. + Sl.Manj."

3. For example, the cèngkok

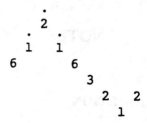

from Gending *Kawit*, pathet manyura, illustrates this difficulty. (For a transcription of that gendhing, see pp. 113–117). The principle of repeatability justifies division of this cèngkok in two ways:

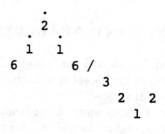

and

Since most pesindhèn usually pause slightly after the second pitch level 6 in this cèngkok, the dividing line has been placed after that pitch level, as in the first cèngkok above.

4. In Figures 9, 11, and 14 I have not indicated the number of times a repeated tone is reiterated. The number of repetitions is unimportant to pathet specification as the following example illustrates. The pathet manyura cèngkok

```
3  3  3  3  3  3         3 /   3
             2  2                2
                 1       1       1
                                    6
                                    .
```

employs six repeated tones, rather than the two repeated tones used in the following pathet manyura cèngkok:

```
   3  3          3 /   3
     2  2               2
         1       1       1
                           6
                           .
```

Since neither of the initial patterns mentioned above is used in pathet sanga, it is clear that the number of repeated tones does not affect the pathet of that cèngkok. In fact, as Gitosaprodjo's notation reveals, these two cèngkok can be sung in the same place in the same gendhing (at the gong marking the end of the first section of Ladrang *Asmara Dana*, pp. 102–3). The longer cèngkok is chosen for a twelve syllable line, rather than the usual eight syllable line.

5. One short initial pattern listed in Figure 14 (2r32r) is eight notes long. It appears in the first cèngkok listed in Figure 29. Despite its length, I have classified this pattern as a short initial pattern because it is very similar to the short initial pattern 2r listed in Figure 14. The latter appears in the second cèngkok in Figure 29. The pitch level 3 in the first pattern in Figure 29 is merely an unimportant trill tone, added for variety in a pattern of repeated notes. Without pitch level 3, this initial pattern is very much like the second initial pattern in Figure 29.

Figure 29. Two Short Initial Patterns

Cèngkok 1, from Ketawang *Kasatriyan*, Sléndro Pathet Sanga
(Sindhèn Cèngkok Notated by Prawotosaputro):

.2 2 2 2 232 2/ .6 21.65

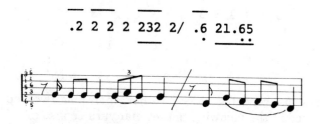

Cèngkok 2, from *Ayak-ayakan*, Sléndro Pathet Sanga
(Sindhèn Cèngkok Sung by Tukinem):

2 2/ 2.6 2 1 6 5

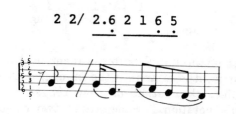

6. All the initial patterns in my corpus of pathet
manyura and pathet sanga gendhing, except two, are listed in
Figures 9 or 14. Those two patterns are not like any of the
initial patterns in Figures 9 and 14. They appear in the
cèngkok given below

```
                   3

        2 2 2   2 /       2
     1       1       1 1   1
                          6 6
```

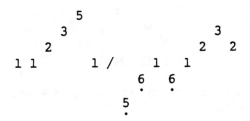

Both of these unusual cèngkok were notated by Ki Wasitodipuro, who is known for his creative innovations in gamelan music. One would expect that in a corpus of some 255 different cèngkok, at least two would not fit into any categories. Thus I have labelled these two initial patterns with question marks in Appendices 2–3.

7. Rules governing the use of plèsèdan cèngkok are not absolutely rigid. Occasionally plèsèdan cèngkok are sung even when immediate repetition of a pitch level in the next gatra does not occur. In that case, the cèngkok ends on a pitch level sounded in the following gatra, even though that pitch level is not repeated. Furthermore, plèsèdan cèngkok sometimes are omitted even if immediate repetition does occur.

8. There is a fourth type of plèsèdan cèngkok but it appears very rarely in my data. The pesindhèn sings a cèngkok of two final patterns.

9. Since the patterns in category 4 occur only six times in my data, the evidence available about category 4 neither contradicts nor supports the theory that pathet sanga cèngkok are lowered one pitch level from pathet manyura cèngkok. Pathet manyura patterns in category 4 are combined with final patterns of pitch levels 6, 1, or 2, whereas pathet sanga patterns are combined with final patterns of pitch level 6.

10. There is one anomalous cèngkok in my data. In Gendhing *Kabor*, sléndro pathet nem, the following cèngkok appears:

$$6$$
$$5 \; / \quad 5$$
$$3 \qquad\qquad 3$$
$$S \quad Sh \quad M \quad Cf$$

The initial pattern is pathet sanga, and the final pattern is pathet manyura.

Chapter 4. PATHET PREDICTION

1. "R. T. Djojodipuro almarhun mengatakan bahwa patet itu ialah tempatnja suatu gending." (The late R. T. Djojodipuro said that pathet is the place of a gendhing.)

2. "Patet dapat berarti menundjukkan tinggi-rendahnja nada2 suatu lagu (gending / tembang)." (Pathet can mean the highness and lowness of the pitches of a piece (in instrumental and in vocal music).)

3. These remarks about the function of gong, kenong, and kempul do not apply to ayak-ayakan, srepegan and sampak, where the gongs operate somewhat differently from the way they do in larger forms (see Becker, Appendix 1:1980). For that reason, neither my study nor the Becker and Templeton study discusses position as a determinant of pathet in ayak-ayakan, srepegan, or sampak. Figures 25 and 31 are based on all the gendhing except for the ayak-ayakan and srepegan listed in Appendices 2, 3, and 4, while Figure 30 is based on all the gendhing in those appendices.

4. The analysis of the information provided by sindhèn contour and pitch level was achieved by using the information formula suggested by Templeton (1980:193–5). The information values for contour were calculated for the six generic contour types, labelled 1, 2, 3 for initial contour, and A, B, C for final contours.

5. The average information for kempul contained in contours for sindhèn patterns in Figure 25 represents a revised average of the information values provided by the six

contour types. If the information values for all six contour types at kempul position are averaged, the figure is .1168. However, I have eliminated two of the information values for the revised average because they are disproportionately high due to unusual features in my sample of thirty gendhing. The two information values I eliminated are contour A (.4307) and contour 3 (.1733). Contour A at kempul position does not even occur once in my data in pathet manyura. With a larger sample, however, contour A in kempul position would probably occur about equally in pathet manyura and pathet sanga. If contour A in kempul position can be shown to occur approximately equally in pathet manyura and pathet sanga, we can predict that it will occur at about the same frequency in pathet nem since pathet nem is a combination of pathet manyura and pathet sanga in terms of sindhèn cèngkok.

The reason for making the above prediction is that contour A patterns occur only with final contours whose last pitch level is 6 in pathet manyura and 5 in pathet sanga; the percentage distribution of these pitch levels at kempul positon in the two pathet directly controls the occurrence of contour A. I will refer to the last pitch level of a gatra in kempul position as a "kempul tone." In my sample, 9.82% of all kempul tones in pathet manyura are pitch level 6, and 23.56% of all kempul tones in pathet sanga are pitch level 5. These two figures differ substantially from percentage distribution of kempul tones taken over a much larger sample (172 gendhing) by Becker and Templeton. According to their data, 18.06% of all kempul tones in pathet manyura are pitch level 6, and 12.98% of all kempul tones in pathet sanga are pitch level 5. (The percentages for kempul were calculated by Templeton, personal communication.) This suggests that the occurrence of contour A in kempul position in pathet manyura and pathet sanga would be close given a larger sample.

For precisely the same reasons, the information value of contour 3 at kempul position is high relative to the other information values. Contour 3 in kempul position in pathet manyura occurs very infrequently in this sample, whereas a larger sample would probably reflect a more equal distribution of contour 3 in kempul position. Like contour A, contour 3 almost always occurs with final contours that end on pitch level 6 in pathet manyura and on pitch level 5 in pathet sanga.

6. This is achieved by determining the range of percentages for pitch levels 3 and 5 in the three pathet over a large number of gendhing (see Figure 30). Thus, in my corpus, pitch level 3 in pathet sanga has the smallest percentage of occurrence in Gendhing *Renyep* (pitch level 3 comprises .81% of all pitch levels sung in that gendhing). The largest percentage for pitch level 3 in pathet sanga occurs in Ladrang *Clunthang*, 12.80%. This range of .81% − 12.80% overlaps only slightly with the manyura range of percentages for pitch level 3, which is 11.49% − 28.57%. See Figure 30 for the ranges for pitch level 5.

Three possible configurations arise when the percentage occurrences of pitch levels 3 and 5 of a gendhing of unknown pathet are calculated. First, if the percentage of occurrence of pitch level 3 falls within the range of the restricted pitch level 3 for pathet sanga (.81% − 12.80%), the gendhing is in pathet sanga. If, however, the percentage occurrence falls in the small area of overlap between the pathet sanga range for pitch level 3 (.81%−12.80%) and the pathet manyura range for pitch level 3 (11.49%−28.57%), then the pathet cannot be determined by looking at pitch level 3. Likewise, if the percentage of occurrence of pitch level 5 falls within the restricted range of pitch level 5 for pathet manyura (3.72%− 12.03%), the piece is in pathet manyura or in pathet nem. (Since pathet nem is more like pathet manyura than like pathet sanga, pitch level 5, but never pitch level 3, is sometimes restricted in pathet nem gendhing. In all the pathet nem gendhing in my sample, the frequency of pitch level 3 never falls within the restricted sanga range of .81%− 12.80%.) Thus, for example, pitch level 5 comprises 9.9% of the pitch levels in Ketawang *Sekar Téja*, pathet manyura.

Figure 30.   Graphic Representation of the Ranges of
Frequencies for pitch Levels 3 and 5 Used in
Sindhèn Cèngkok in All Gendhing in the Three
Sléndro Pathet

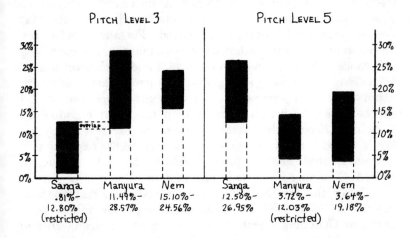

This percentage falls within the range of the restricted pitch
level 5 for pathet manyura (3.72% – 12.03%) and also within
the range for pathet nem, but not within the range for pathet
sanga.

Secondly, if the percentage falls outside of any of the
ranges, it is usually clear to what pathet the gendhing
belongs. If the percentage of pitch level 3 is higher than any
of the ranges, the pathet is either manyura or nem.
Similarly, if the percentage of pitch level 5 is higher than any
of the ranges, the pathet is probably sanga. If the frequencies of pitch levels 3 or 5 are lower than the sanga or
manyura ranges respectively, then the pathet is sanga or
manyura respectively, since pitch levels 3 and 5 are
restricted in pathet sanga and manyura respectively. For
example, in Ketawang *Sekar Téja*, the percentage of occurrence of pitch level 3 (31.80%) is higher than any of the

ranges for pitch level 3 (11.49% — 28.57%). Thus the gendhing is in pathet manyura or pathet nem, since pitch level 3 is not restricted in these two pathet.

Thirdly, if pitch levels 3 and 5 are about the same frequency, probably the gendhing is in pathet nem, since about equal frequencies of pitch levels 3 and 5 indicate that neither pitch level 3 nor 5 is restricted. For almost all of the pathet manyura and pathet sanga gendhing in my data, the difference in percentage of pitch level 3 and pitch level 5 is at least 7%. Of course, judging that two percentage points are about equal is a somewhat subjective procedure, but it still can be used as a rough measure of pathet. For example, in Gendhing *Kocak*, the percentages of occurrence for pitch levels 3 and 5 are very close (14.3% and 16.8% respectively) indicating that neither pitch level 3 nor 5 is restricted. Indeed, Gendhing *Kocak* is in pathet nem.

Using this method, I have correctly determined that Ketawang *Sekar Téja* is in pathet manyura or pathet nem, and that Gendhing *Kocak* is in pathet nem. Ladrang *Dirada Meta* is either in pathet manyura or pathet nem, since both the low occurrence of pitch level 5 (8.3%) and the high occurrence of pitch level 3 (22.6%) exclude pathet sanga.

7. The average information for pitch level per sindhèn pattern is higher at gong position for several reasons. First, on the average, sindhèn patterns at gong position are longer than at kenong or kempul positions, and thus the accumulated information values are higher. Secondly, the information values for pitch levels 1, 2, and 3 are higher at gong position than at the other positions (see Figure 31). This can be illustrated by the pattern

$$2$$
$$1$$
$$\underset{\bullet}{6} \quad \underset{\bullet}{6}$$
$$\underset{\bullet}{5}$$

The pitch information provided by this pattern at gong position is .1333, while at kenong position it is only .0519. Pitch levels 1 and 2 are common and often reiterated in cèngkok that end on pitch level 5 in pathet sanga, while pitch level 3 is very common in cèngkok that end on pitch level 6 in pathet manyura. The ending note of a cèngkok is dictated by the end-pitch of the saron gatra. Saron gatra ending on pitch level 5 in pathet sanga and pitch level 6 in pathet manyura are more common in gong position than in kenong or kempul position. In addition, pitch level 3 is often used as a reduplicated tone to accommodate long poetic lines in pathet manyura, while in pathet sanga, pitch level 2 is used for this purpose. Long poetic lines are more frequently found at gong position than at kenong or kempul position.

Figure 31. Information with Respect to Sléndro Pathet Contained in Pitch Levels of Sindhèn Patterns in Each of the Three Positons in the Gong Cycle

Pitch Level	Gong	Kenong	Kempul
1	.0191	.0081	.0089
2	.0063	.0027	.0013
3	.1601	.0566	.0066
5	.0662	.0703	.0412
6	.0031	.0026	.0025

Chapter 5. DIFFERENT SYSTEMS OF PATHET IN THE GAMELAN

1. "Djadi seandainja ladrang Pangkur Slendro patet Manjura dan patet Sanga, mungkin lagu vocalnja akan sama, tetapi instrumentalianja tentu mengalami perbedaan. Hal ini turbukti, bila kita beladjar bonang. Teknik bonangan Pangkur patet Manjura tidak akan berdaja dalam menghadapi patet Sanga jang artinja tidak hanja digeser kebawah atau keatas belaka (seperti pada pengertian transposisi pada musik Barat)."

2. "Pernah ada pertanjaan berhubung tidak mungkinnja membuat tjengkok baru, bagai mana kalau tjengkok-2 lama itu dinaik-turunkan sadja (transposisi); djawab saja: 'Kami jakin tetap sukar.' Bila dari tjengkok manjura misalnja, masih mungkin untuk ditransposisikan ke patet Sanga dengan menurunkan nada-2nja satu bilah namun kadang-2 masih harus ada jang dipaksakan."

3. Of course not all pathet manyura rebab cèngkok can be lowered one pitch level to produce pathet sanga cèngkok, because of the fingering limitations of a two-stringed instrument.

4. Diverse concepts operating in a single context is the basis of Hoffman's notion of "multiple epistemologies" (1975 and 1978). The concept of "inner melody" (Sumarsam, 1975 and 1984) is another example: just as different instruments in the gamelan have different systems of pathet, they also have their own idiomatic performance styles to realize a basic inner melody. Sutton (1975) also discusses inner melody, for which he uses the Javanese term *lagu*. Another example of the Javanese acceptance of opposing systems within one context is the use of *barang miring cèngkok*, in which rebab, dhalang, and pesindhèn sound pitches totally foreign to laras sléndro, even while the other instruments in the gamelan are playing normal sléndro cèngkok. For an example of a barang miring cèngkok, see Appendix 1. In the cultural sphere, the Javanese tolerate a great variety of personality types, ethical

codes, and physical body types, as exemplified by their love of the many different mythological characters of the wayang world (Anderson 1969:25–6). There are even four calendrical systems which operate simultaneously: an indigenous system of five and seven day weeks, the Indian Saka Era, the Islamic lunar calendar, and the Christian calendar.

5. It is difficult to know whether to classify the slenthem as a loud-sounding instrument or as a soft-sounding instrument. It is played in the otherwise exclusively soft-sounding ensemble, the *gamelan gadhon*. Yet it is also played in many loud style gendhing. In describing the loud and soft-sounding instruments in a nineteenth-century gamelan, Kartomi (*ca.* 1974:5) classifies the slenthem as a loud-sounding instrument.

6. According to Hardja Susilo (personal communication), *gendhing talèdhèkan* refers only to a particular kind of performance style which imitates the style used in the talèdhèk's music. This style can be used for any gendhing. Thus, gendhing talèdhèkan did not necessarily accompany the dance of the talèdhèk. Kunst and Ki Wasitodipuro, however, seem to disagree with Susilo on this point.

7. According to Sastrapustaka and Ki Wasitodipuro (both personal communications), however, the talèdhèk was accompanied by kendhang and bonang. If this is so, the voice, which I have regarded as a soft-sounding instrument, was associated with a loud-sounding instrument even before the talèdhèk started singing in the full gamelan.

8. Although evidence for determining the instrumental accompaniment of wayang in past centuries is scant, the following three points suggests that the saron was not part of that accompaniment: (1) *Wayang bèbèr*, a form of wayang at least as old if not older than wayang kulit, is accompanied only by rebab, kendhang, *rebana* (a frame drum), *angklung* (a bamboo xylophone), and keprak (a small slit drum made of wood and struck with a wooden mallet) (Sastroamidjojo 1964(?):84). According to another source (a wayang bèbèr recording from Karangtalun by Martin Hatch, 1969), the

accompaniment consists of rebab, kendhang, kenong, kethuk, kempul and gong. (2) Balinese wayang is accompanied only by a gendèr quartet. (3) The fifth stanza from canto 50 of *The Kakawin Bharata-Yuddha* by mpu Seddah and mpu Panuluh suggests that gendèr, flutes, and female singers comprised wayang accompaniment in the twelfth century. See Kunst (1968:76–7) for a detailed discussion of this stanza. Incidentally, the "female singers" do not refer to pesindhèn here (Kunst 1968:77).

REFERENCES

PART A: WORKS CITED

Anderson, Benedict R. 1965. *Mythology and the Tolerance of the Javanese*. Ithaca, New York: Cornell Modern Indonesia Project, Monograph Series.

Becker, Judith. 1980. *Traditional Music in Modern Java: Gamelan in a Changing Society*. Honolulu: University Press of Hawaii.

Darmoredjono, Kenang. 1968. *Gending Djawi Sekarsari* (Javanese Gendhing: The Essence of Poetry). Wonogiri, Indonesia: Jawatan Penerangan Kabupaten Wonogiri.

Gitosaprodjo, Sulaiman. 1970. "Peladjaran Dasar Gender" (A Beginning Study Course for the Gendèr). Manuscript. Malang, Indonesia.

————.1970b. "Peladjaran Dasar Rebab" (A Beginning Study Course for the Rebab). Manuscript. Malang, Indonesia.

————.1971a. *Ichtisar Teori Karawitan dan Teknik Menabuh Gamelan* (A Summary of the Theory of Music and the Technique of Playing the Gamelan). Published in stencil form. Malang, Indonesia: Keluarga Karawitan Studio RRI Malang.

————.1971b. *Ichtisar Teori Sindenan* (A Summary of the Theory of Solo Female Singing). Published in stencil form. Malang, Indoneisa.

————.1971c. "Suling Karawitan Sala" (Flute Playing in the Solonese Gamelan). Manuscript. Malang, Indonesia.

————.1972a. *Teori dan Praktek Gerong* (Theory and Practice of Male Choral Singing), vol.1. Published in stencil form. Malang, Indonesia: Keluarga Karawitan Studio RRI Malang.

————.1972b. *Titilaras Gending* (Gendhing Notation), vol. 1. Malang, Indonesia: Pertiwi Cabang Kota Madya Malang.

————.1984. "Ichtisar Teori Karawitan dan Teknik Menabuh Gamelan." Translation from the Indonesian by Judith Becker in *Karawitan: Source Readings in Javanese Gamelan and Vocal Music*, vol.1, edited by Judith Becker, 335–387. Michigan Papers in South and Southeast Asian Studies no 23. Ann Arbor, Michigan: Center for South and Southeast Asian Studies.

————.No Date a. *Pelengkap Teori Sindenan* (Complete Theory of Solo Female Singing). Published in stencil form. Malang, Indonesia: Pertiwi Cabang Kota Madya Malang.

————.No Date b. "Sindenan Titilaras Tjakepan" (Notation and Texts for Solo Female Singing) vols. 1–2. Manuscript. Malang, Indonesia.

Hoffman, Stanley Brian. 1975. "Epistemology and Music in Java." Master's thesis, Ann Arbor, Michigan.

————.1978. "Epistemology and Music: A Javanese Example." *Ethnomusicology*, vol. 22, no. 1 (January):69–88.

Hood, Mantle. 1954. *The Nuclear Theme as a Determinant of Patet in Javanese Music*. Groningen and Jakarta: J. B. Wolters.

Ijzerdraat, Bernard. 1959. "Rhythm and Dance in Java." In *Tari dan Kesusasteran di Djawa* (Dance and Literature in Java) edited by Koentjaraningrat, pp.13–15. Jogjakarta: Percetakan Taman Siswa.

Kartomi, Margaret. *Ca.* 1974. "Music in Nineteenth Century Java." Manuscript.

References

Kunst, Jaap. 1968. *Hindu-Javanese Musical Instruments* (second edition). The Hague: Martinus Nijhoff.

————.1973. *Music in Java : Its History, Its Theory and Its Technique.* Edited by Ernst Heins. 3rd edition, 2 vols. The Hague: Martinus Nijhoff.

Martopangrawit, R.L. 1969. *Catatan-catatan Pengetahuan Karawitan* (Notes on the Knowledge of Gamelan). Vol.1. Surakarta, Indonesia: Akademi Seni Karawitan Indonesia. Typescript.

————.1972. "Catatan-catatan Pengetahuan Karawitan" Vol.2. Surakarta, Indonesia: Seni Karawitan Indonesia. Typescript.

————.1984. "Catatan-catatan Pengetahuan Karawitan," Vols.I and II. Translation from the Indonesian by Martin Hatch in *Karawitan: Source Readings in Javanese Gamelan and Vocal Music*, vol.1, edited by Judith Becker, 1–244. Michigan Papers in South and Southeast Asian Studies no. 23. Ann Arbor, Michigan: Center for South and Southeast Asian Studies.

Martopangrawit, R.L., and Sumarsam. 1971. "Gerong Bedayan" (Mixed Male Female Choral Singing). Surakarta, Indonesia: Akademi Seni Karawitan Indonesia. Typescript.

McDermott, Vincent, and Sumarsam. 1975. "Central Javanese Music: The Patet of Laras Sléndro and the Gendèr Barung." *Ethnomusicology*, vol. 19, no. 2 (May):233–244.

Pakubuwana X. 1926. *Noot Gending lan Tembang* (Gendhing and Tembang Notation). Surabaya, Indonesia: Percetakan Nasional.

————.Forthcoming. "Noot Gending lan Tembang." Translation from the Indonesian by Hardja Susilo in *Karawitan: Source Readings in Javanese Gamelan and Vocal Music*, vol.2, edited by Judith Becker. Michigan Papers in South and Southeast Asia. Ann Arbor, Michigan: Center for South and Southeast Asian Studies.

Pigeaud, Th. G. Th. 1967. *Literature of Java*. Vol. 1. The Hague: Martinus Nijhoff.

————.1938. *Javaans-Nederlands Handwoordenboek* (Javanese-Dutch Dictionary). Groningen and Batavia: J.B. Wolters' Uitgevers-Maatschappij.

Prawotosaputro. 1969. "Ketawang *Kasatriyan*." manuscript.

Probohardjono, R. Ng. S. 1957. *Gending-gending ingkang kangge Nabuhi Wayangan Purwa* (Gamelan Pieces for Accompanying Shadow Theater). Yogyakarta, Indonesia: Usaha Penerbitan P.T. Sinduniti.

Purbodiningrat, R. T. 1956. "Gamelan." *Sana-Budaja 1* (Journal on Indonesian Culture) no. 4:185–206.

————.Forthcoming. "Gamelan." Translation from the Indonesian by Stanley Hoffman in *Karawitan: Source Readings in Javanese Gamelan and Vocal Music*, vol.2, edited by Judith Becker. Michigan Papers in South and Southeast Asia. Ann Arbor, Michigan: Center for South and Southeast Asian Studies.

Sastroamidjojo, Dr. Seno. 1964(?). *Renungan tentang Pertundjukan Wajang Kulit* (Relections on a Wayang Kulit Performance). Jakartv, Indonesia: P.T. Kinta.

Solheim, Wilhelm G. 1971. "New Light on a Forgotten Past." *National Geographic* 139:330–39.

Sumarsam. 1975. "Inner Melody in Javanese Gamelan Music." *Asian Music*, vol.7, no. 1:3–13.

————.1984. "Inner Melody in Javanese Gamelan." In *Karawitan Source Readings in Javanese Gamelan and Vocal Music*, vol. 1, ed. by Judith Becker, 245–304. Michigan Papers on South and Southeast Asia no. 23. Ann Arbor, Michigan: Center for South and Southeast Asian Studies.

Sutton, R. Anderson. 1975. "The Javanese Gambang and Its Music." Master's thesis, University of Hawaii.